Quick Guide

PATIOS & WALKS

CREATIVE HOMEOWNER PRESS®

Creative Director: Warren Ramezzana
Editor: Arnie Edelstein
Project Editor: Kimberly Kerrigone
Graphic Designer: Annie Jeon
Illustrators: James Randolph, Norman Nuding
Production Assistant: Mindy Circelli
Technical Reviewer: Jim Barrett

Cover Design: Warren Ramezzana
Cover Illustrations: Moffit Cecil

Electronic Prepress: M. E. Aslett Corporation
Printed at: Quebecor Printing Inc.

Current Printing (last digit)
10 9 8 7 6 5 4 3

Quick Guide: Patios & Walks
LC: 92-81620
ISBN: 1-880029-07-3 (paper)

CREATIVE HOMEOWNER PRESS®
A Division of Federal Marketing Corp.
24 Park Way
Upper Saddle River, NJ 07458

C O N T E N T S

SAFETY FIRST

Though all the designs and methods in this book have been tested for safety, it is not possible to overstate the importance of using the safest construction methods possible. What follows are reminders; some do's and don'ts of basic carpentry. They are not substitutes for your own common sense.

- *Always* use caution, care, and good judgment when following the procedures described in this book.

- *Always* be sure that the electrical setup is safe; be sure that no circuit is overloaded, and that all power tools and electrical outlets are properly grounded. Do not use power tools in wet locations.

- *Always* read container labels on paints, solvents, and other products; provide ventilation, and observe all other warnings.

- *Always* read the tool manufacturer's instructions for using a tool, especially the warnings.

- *Always* use holders or pushers to work pieces shorter than 3 inches on a table saw or jointer. Avoid working short pieces if you can.

- *Always* remove the key from any drill chuck (portable or press) before starting the drill.

- *Always* pay deliberate attention to how a tool works so that you can avoid being injured.

- *Always* know the limitations of your tools. Do not try to force them to do what they were not designed to do.

- *Always* make sure that any adjustment is locked before proceeding. For example, always check the rip fence on a table saw or the bevel adjustment on a portable saw before starting to work.

- *Always* clamp small pieces firmly to a bench or other work surfaces when sawing or drilling.

- *Always* wear the appropriate rubber or work gloves when handling chemicals, heavy construction or when sanding.

- *Always* wear a disposable mask when working with odors, dusts or mists. Use a special respirator when working with toxic substances.

- *Always* wear eye protection, especially when using power tools or striking metal on metal or concrete; a chip can fly off, for example, when chiseling concrete.

- *Always* be aware that there is never time for your body's reflexes to save you from injury from a power tool in a dangerous situation; everything happens too fast. Be *alert!*

- *Always* keep your hands away from the business ends of blades, cutters and bits.

- *Always* hold a portable circular saw with both hands so that you will know where your hands are.

- *Always* use a drill with an auxiliary handle to control the torque when large size bits are used.

- *Always* check your local building codes when planning new construction. The codes are intended to protect public safety and should be observed to the letter.

- *Never* work with power tools when you are tired or under the influence of alcohol or drugs.

- *Never* cut very small pieces of wood or pipe. Whenever possible, cut small pieces off larger pieces.

- *Never* change a blade or a bit unless the power cord is unplugged. Do not depend on the switch being off; you might accidentally hit it.

- *Never* work in insufficient lighting.

- *Never* work while wearing loose clothing, hanging hair, open cuffs, or jewelry.

- *Never* work with dull tools. Have them sharpened, or learn how to sharpen them yourself.

- *Never* use a power tool on a workpiece that is not firmly supported or clamped.

- *Never* saw a workpiece that spans a large distance between horses without close support on either side of the kerf; the piece can bend, closing the kerf and jamming the blade, causing saw kickback.

- *Never* support a workpiece with your leg or other part of your body when sawing.

- *Never* carry sharp or pointed tools, such as utility knives, awls, or chisels in your pocket. If you want to carry tools, use a special-purpose tool belt with leather pockets and holders.

DESIGN CHECKLIST

A patio is an extension of your indoor living space—
an "outdoor room." Before beginning patio
construction, undertake a thorough investigation of the
elements that will influence the shape and fit of the
patio. Most likely, the biggest questions to answer are:

■ What do you want from your patio?

■ How is it to be used?

■ Will its purpose be to extend an overused room?

Functional Considerations

A well-designed outdoor space, large or small, should be almost entirely determined before any physical construction begins. By answering the question, "What do I want from an outdoor room?" you initiate the ideas that will lead to a successful design solution. Consider whether you want a very formal outdoor area primarily for entertaining larger groups or a space for informally entertaining small groups. Will the area be used for sunbathing or will it be located next to a swimming pool? Will you need space accessible for the handicapped or the very elderly? Is it to be completely secure from the outside? Is privacy a priority item on your checklist? If so, it might mean that the area must be fenced in or enclosed by trees or shrubs in arrangements that will prevent invasion of the patio.

After answering these questions, as well as the ones listed below, and carefully evaluating your lifestyle, you can choose what type of outdoor space you want and how it will best suit your needs.

How Are Your Present Living Spaces Used? In answering this question, keep in mind that a patio is most often located near a kitchen area or family room. Another popular location is near or adjacent to the dining room. The location should be near the largest traffic flow in the house. It also should be an area that can be modified easily without drastically changing the everyday operations of the household. Proximity to a kitchen often assures an easy flow of food and beverages without excessive footwear. Less frequently, one sees a small private patio off a bedroom or bathroom.

How Large a Patio Do I Need? To give a blanket size does not take into account individual needs. Recommended dimensions provide for 20 square feet per person—a space that is comfortable without

Functional Considerations. A patio can divide the backyard into separate areas for a variety of activities.

being excessive. This converts to an area of 4x5 feet, and includes a chair and area in which to circulate. If you contemplate entertaining a group of 15 to 25 people, the corresponding size in area would be: 500 square feet or an equivalent size of 20 feet by 25 feet. Keep in mind that there are limits to what a reasonably sized patio can hold. If the immediate area around the contemplated patio is accessible for larger groups, you might find that a smaller patio will function far more efficiently than a grandiose one. Be realistic about the space needed. Often a clever arrangement of furniture or plants will give the impression of a much larger space and yet retain the charm of a more intimate area. Where much larger groups than 15 to 25 are contemplated, the patio must be situated so as to take advantage of your site. This will handle overflow without overcrowding.

How Will I Use the Patio? First decide whether you need a formal or informal area. A patio subjected to considerable wear and tear caused by children or pets must be sturdy while remaining suitable for adults.

An informal arrangement requires less attention to design details. Built-in furniture provides seating and reduces the amount of outdoor furniture that must be purchased. The units remain fixed and are not as susceptible to damage. In a formal patio, more fragile materials might be used—along with delicate flower borders, trellises, slate or cobblestones.

Is Privacy a Concern? The openness of a patio is most often determined by the degree of privacy desired. While there are other determinants (see pages 10-11 and 17-20) that will affect this decision, the need for privacy often dictates the final design solution. Keep in mind that there are three types of privacy:

■ visual privacy;

■ acoustical privacy;

■ physical privacy.

Identification of the three types is important because you may be concerned with one, two or all three. Each type requires a specific architectural treatment.

Visual Privacy. You may discover that the most desirable exposure for the patio may face an unsightly yard or street—not to mention the houses or apartments nearby that can easily peer into your yard. To correct this and gain visual privacy, several recommendations follow.

■ A simple wood fence, high enough to screen out the undesirable view, or a low brick or decorative concrete block wall, often creates an effective screen.

■ Rows of shrubs of varying height will limit the view into and out of the space.

■ A lattice covered with ivy is an effective screen technique.

■ For those sites where protection from above is desired, a trellis roof with vines should be considered, although it may reduce the light level.

■ A wood roof structure with inserted translucent plastic or fiberglass panels guarantees a high level of privacy from any overhead viewing.

Acoustical Privacy. Do you wish to eliminate or tone down unwanted or bothersome noises? While no method can provide acoustical isolation, using readily available materials and landscaping, can offer some relief from distracting noise.

■ The best method uses layers of shrubs or evergreens. For example, evergreens placed in rows perpendicular to the noise source will break up the noise so it will merge with other background noises.

■ An urban or suburban lot will require more privacy than an isolated country site. A fence, in combination with vertical evergreens or shrubs, will give additional isolation from noise sources that are exceptionally severe.

■ Since it is impossible to stop all noise from penetrating your outdoor area, keep in mind that a patio is, by its nature, open. The greater the closure of the area, the more likely that it will lose its flexibility and desirability.

Physical Privacy. Another term for physical privacy is "security." There may be a need to detain intruders such as uninvited guests or pets. While fences with controlled access or lockable gates can prevent strangers from wandering in off the street, low walls with evergreens or dense shrubs may provide all the security you need. When evaluating your specific needs, determine:

■ whether a controlled access to the outdoor area is needed;

■ what kind of security is required— this will partially depend on whether or not the patio is enclosed in any manner;

■ whether you need a method of keeping youngsters out of (or inside) the area.

If you have a swimming pool adjacent to the patio, your "attractive nuisance" should exist inside a secure fence.

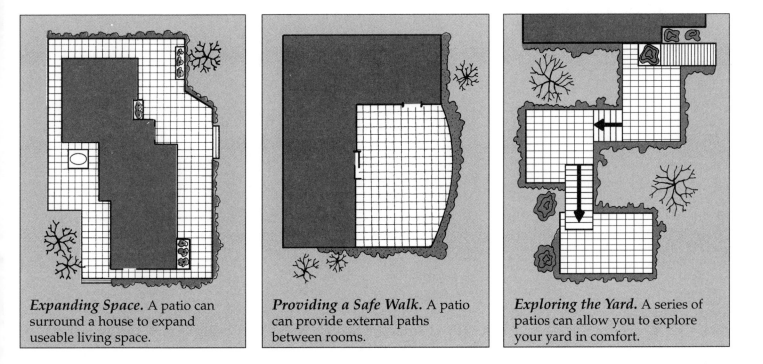

Expanding Space. A patio can surround a house to expand useable living space.

Providing a Safe Walk. A patio can provide external paths between rooms.

Exploring the Yard. A series of patios can allow you to explore your yard in comfort.

Site Considerations

Now that you have identified what you want from an outdoor room, the next step in evaluating your needs is to understand the physical and environmental limitations of the site. These restrictions have as much influence over the physical design as your functional requirements. It is essential to the success of your patio that you evaluate the following considerations.

Terrain. The location of the patio you choose to build may be dictated by the terrain. A flat area of ground just off the kitchen or family room is obviously suitable for a patio. However, if the terrain is excessively pitched either to the house or away from the house, the project will become costly.

The effect of the slope of terrain in relation to the level of your house is very important.

Generally a five or six percent slope is quite acceptable for the construction of a patio. If the ground slopes into the house rather than away from it, you will have to raise the patio surface higher than you would for ground that slopes away, no matter what material you choose.

If there is a portion of the site that is quite steep, while the majority of it is flat or gently sloping, a retaining wall may be needed. If the retaining wall is a steep vertical embankment (three feet or higher), it will usually prove beyond the abilities of the do-it-yourselfer, since a few harsh winters will cause the materials to give way. Shorter or stepped-back walls of boulders or railroad ties are sufficient for slope control at heights of three feet or less.

Plants and Trees. In planning an outdoor space, inventory the existing plants and trees found in the areas under consideration. Evaluate the relative condition and the survival ability of each plant or tree to be moved to an alternate location. To move a mature tree that is located

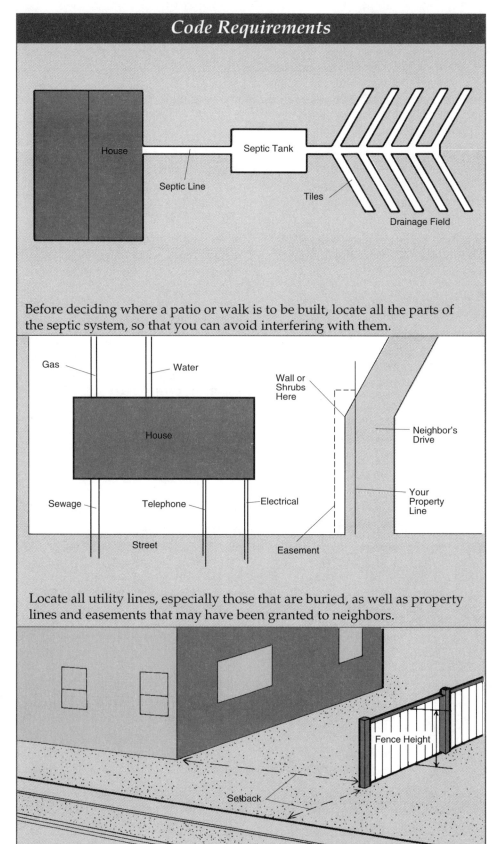

Code Requirements

Before deciding where a patio or walk is to be built, locate all the parts of the septic system, so that you can avoid interfering with them.

Locate all utility lines, especially those that are buried, as well as property lines and easements that may have been granted to neighbors.

Local codes may restrict the locations and dimensions of fences, patios, overheads and walks, in relation to the street or to next-door neighbors.

where you want the patio is impractical, and cutting the tree down is not a good solution. Rather than cut a mature tree down, the patio design can be constructed to include the tree. This is most often done by leaving an opening around the trunk. Keep in mind that a minimum of transplanting and cutting is the most satisfactory course; this reduces your total replacement costs.

Once a location has been chosen, check off those plants or trees that can be kept and those that must be moved. Your local nursery or landscaper should be consulted if you are unsure of a particular plant's hardiness.

Utilities. Prior to building a patio, it is very important to determine the location of all underground utilities. Water, gas, sewage and telephone lines can influence the position of outdoor construction either by requiring special construction or relocation of the lines or the patio.

Many accidents have occurred as a result of not knowing where the lines were located, and at what depth in the ground. To locate these utility lines, check with your local utility companies through their customer-service department. They will help you determine the specific location of their service and also may suggest ways of building over or around the problem. If your house was built recently, your local building inspector should have a copy of your utility, gas, water and sewage hookup locations.

This information should be kept in your files for future reference. You may discover that no connections or underground lines exist under the proposed patio. However, if there is a conflict, consult with the service in question or your local building inspector in order to explore the options. Most often, the utilities are located in a zone from 2 1/2 feet to 8 feet in depth. Normally, the major concern is that the location of deep footings or retaining walls will conflict with the utility service.

Codes. Building codes were established to protect the public's health and safety. They originally were developed to insure that all safety requirements and loadings were within reasonable and realistic limits. The building codes in use today are much more specific.

Prior to any construction, a building permit must be obtained. To obtain one, contact your local building inspector's office. This office may require a set of plans (see pages 17-20). In their review of your plan, they will make sure that your proposal meets all applicable codes. Once the permit is awarded, you may begin construction.

Zoning. Zoning codes were created to control land usage and the density of building in any one area. Zoning regulations indicate the setback requirements. These requirements determine how closely you may build to your property lines, how high fences or trellises may be, and in some cases, what materials may be used. Your local building inspector

will be able to furnish you with the necessary information.

Determine if any easements are located on your property. These rights of way might limit the building of your patio. Your property deed should indicate if any easements are in force.

Soil Conditions. While soil conditions around your house are most often stable, it is important to keep in mind that minor excavation should be filled in as soon as possible to reduce settlement of the slab or supports. Generally, soils with a large clay content tend to swell during the spring; causing the patio to move. By introducing construction joints in the patio, movement is controlled easily. Most other types of soil are considered quite stable for the support of a patio.

Pools. If you are planning to have ornamental or reflecting pools as part of your design, locating the closest water supply source is important. Try to minimize the amount of pipe required to service the pool. In Northern climates, insure that the pipe can be pitched from a high to low level so it can be drained.

Electrical Needs. Electrical service for power outlets and/or lighting also must be determined well in advance of the construction. Underground service from your power panel, or through-the-wall service, should be considered in your location of the patio. It is important to minimize the degree of difficulty for the electrical service connection.

Climatic Considerations

This section covers environmental and physical factors that will affect the amount and type of light, the volume and direction of wind, and the control of rain or snowfall on your patio design. An exterior space that is oriented solely for a view might become unusable if the elements are not taken into account. The following list will assist you in understanding the basics of environmental design.

Orientation. This involves deciding what direction your planned outdoor living area will face; a factor which will affect the amount of sun and shade received.

A north-facing space in the Northern Hemisphere will primarily be in shade most of the day. This is the most desirable exposure in a Southern climate, but could be cold and uncomfortable in Northern climates. In a Southern climate, the next-best orientation is an easterly exposure, so that the morning sun falls on the outdoor area. In colder or more severe climates, to make outdoor spaces useable as long as possible, a southwest exposure provides full afternoon and late afternoon sun. This results in a warmer outdoor area on many cooler spring and fall days.

The activities you are planning for the patio can influence its orientation. Sunlight may or may not be a desirable factor, depending upon the climate. It is up to you to evaluate your own specific needs regarding the quality of light needed. Northern light tends to be far more diffused than direct sunlight. Understanding that difference can influence your plans for the level of sunlight.

The position of the sun in the sky, and the angle of the sun, also are worth considering. During the summer months, the angle of the sun is higher than in the winter. This means that during the winter months a southern-oriented patio will receive

Summer

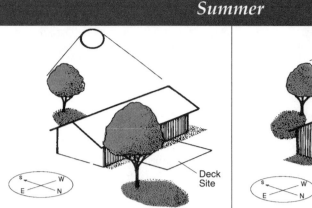

In the Northern Hemisphere, the noonday summer sun stands high in the sky; buildings and trees cast little shadow.

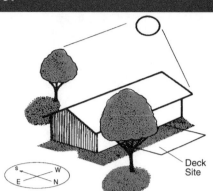

The late afternoon summer sun is as far to the north as it will go; there will be minimal shade on the north and east of buildings.

Spring & Autumn

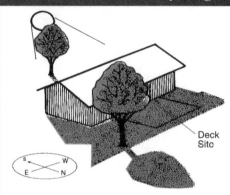

The noonday sun in spring and autumn is partway to its zenith; buildings cast considerable shadows, as do fully-leafed trees.

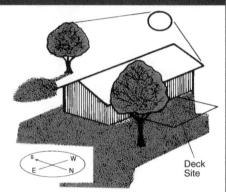

The late afternoon spring and autumn sun is fairly low in the sky; there is much shadow on the north and east sides of buildings.

Winter

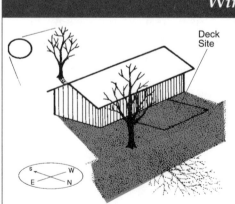

The winter sun is at its lowest point; buildings cast the deepest north-side shadows of the year; leafless trees cast none at all.

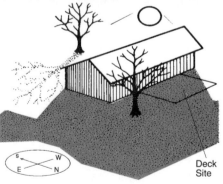

The afternoon winter sun stands low and to the south; buildings cast very deep shadows to the north and east sides.

less direct sunlight than during the summer months. If you are considering a fence or other obstacle on the southern side of the patio, there is the possibility that very little sun will penetrate during the winter months. However, sunlight will fall across most of the surface of the outdoor area during the summer. Especially in the Southern regions, overhead trellises or lanais are used as sunscreens to permit a controlled amount of light. In Northern climates they may offer too much shade.

Wind. In excess, wind can create a very uncomfortable or even unusable patio, even if all the other conditions are just right. Planning to accommodate the wind's movements means that you must observe the wind pattern around your house. Try to recall where leaves collect in the fall; this might indicate a zone that has little air movement. If the site experiences a constant breeze over the entire day, some form of windbreak is in order.

In a Southern climate, air movement is considered a definite advantage. Air moving under a screening or a shading device will feel cooler than when exposed to direct sunlight. The temperature is about the same, but the moving air gives a cooling sensation. A sunshade can in fact aid in the cooling of the interior of the house, even though situated outside. Depending on the location of the sunshade, preferably on the windward side of the house this cooling effect can be achieved. Evaluate the position of the patio in terms of the day breeze and the night air movement. If you are fortunate enough to have a consistent wind pattern during the day, position the area to take advantage of it. Breezes are easily directed and controlled. In zones where the air movement is minimal, locate the patio in a position where the air will be funneled through the patio and amplified.

Types of Patio Ventilation

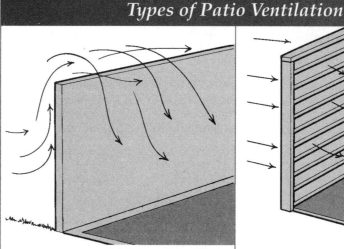

A solid wall deflects most breezes over the patio, while allowing gentle ventilation near the wall.

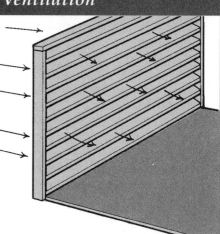

A louvered wall lets all air currents through to the patio; slanting the louvers up or down can direct the breezes as you desire.

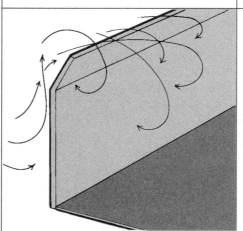

A solid wall with an inward-angled extension draws air currents down, creating movement near the wall.

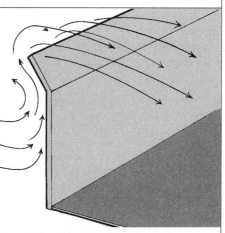

A solid wall with an outward-angled extension deflects air currents up and over the patio, creating a still area near the wall.

Panels in an acrylic-walled patio can be hinged to permit any desired degree of ventilation by prevailing winds.

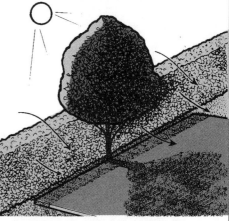

Shrubbery and trees will deflect and moderate prevailing winds, allowing some gentle ventilation of patio areas.

Rain. Rain falling on a patio can have interesting consequences. If the patio has not been pitched to shed the water, ponding or puddling is produced. The result, in some cases, is minor flooding—especially if the patio is on the same level as the house. This is why it is wise to lower the patio several inches. Keep in mind that all horizontal surfaces should be pitched away from the house no less than an 1/8 inch per foot. A 1/4 inch per foot slope is best for most outdoor areas, as it provides positive drainage even in the heaviest of rain. If the proposed patio is 10 feet wide, it should drop from the house side to the outside edge by about 2½ inches, in order to minimize any flooding or ponding. Be sure that the adjacent area is capable of handling the concentrated rain accumulated by the patio, or you may wash out in areas you had not anticipated.

Snow. The effects of snow are similar to the effects of rain in the weathering of the patio.

All materials will tend to deteriorate under the influence of weathering. Your outdoor area and the materials will naturally change over the years.

Each material has its own patina of weathering. A well-selected grouping of materials may appear visually incompatible during construction, but after several years of exposure to the elements will blend together in a most pleasing manner. Find samples of materials that already have weathered. Select based on what it will look like two years from now rather than tomorrow, when it is first built.

Freezing and Thawing. Northern climates, where freezing and thawing occur, have the potential for the greatest damage to building materials. Concrete slabs will crack and heave if not properly constructed and reinforced. These problems are caused by the freezing of tiny particles of water which expand when frozen. It is imperative that you select materials appropriate to your climate. You must control the method of construction enough to minimize the risk of disaster due to freezing and thawing. Sufficiently thick slabs and footings, and expansion joints will reduce the cracking of concrete due to frost heaving (see page 23).

Creating the Design

The functional, site, and climatic considerations discussed above take into account physical realities that influence your plans. The design ideas and methods offer a means of converting your needs and desires into physical design solutions. The opportunity still exists, in this process, to modify or reevaluate your plan simply by altering your original criteria and their requirements.

While there are many ideas and possibilities available, the choice of material will strongly influence your design options. A strong geometric material such as brick, for example, is not very easily integrated into a circular motif.

Try to keep your selection limited to no more than two materials. Use of a wide variety of materials can lead to overly complex and poorly executed construction. By restricting the materials to no more than two types, you will discover that you have greater flexibility in the actual construction of the patio and in the final outfitting of the area. Even a single material will give you a very effective overall look if combined with outdoor furniture and flowers.

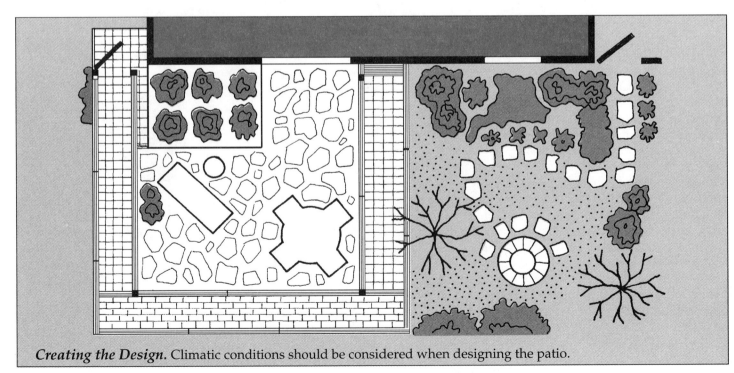

Creating the Design. Climatic conditions should be considered when designing the patio.

Choosing a Material

A patio, because it is usually built on or into a prepared ground level, allows for a great range of material choices. Choosing a material means finding a surface material that fits the colors and the architectural design of your house, as well as the overall feeling of the outdoor area. It calls for use of locally available materials and, whenever possible, materials that require minimum maintenance.

Brick

Brick fits in almost anywhere. It evokes feelings of solidity, warmth, permanence and economic well-being. Brick is widely available and is competitively priced with other patio building materials. The coloration of brick is extensive, from yellow ochres to deep earth browns and blacks. The textural qualities vary from smooth to rough or grainy. Brick is a relatively easy material to handle, yet it provides a decorative effect that appears complex. New, used or salvaged brick can be pleasing in a variety of patio designs. Bricks that have a ceramic coating on one face can be used as a highlight element or in high traffic areas. The ceramic coating comes in a large range of colors to complement the regular brick pattern.

Concrete

Concrete has become a universal material. It can be used in a variety of ways and in many types of construction. It has few design limitations and can be self-supporting if necessary. Due to its visual hardness, concrete does not fit into all designs well. It best suits a contemporary scheme.

There are many kinds of concrete finishes available. Depending on the desired effect and usage, it can be finished in a very flat, smooth style, or a very rough surface with an uneven texture. Most concrete patios are constructed on a well-prepared and tamped gravel base. The concrete is then poured over the gravel base to the desired thickness. It is at this time that additional materials may be inserted or a surface pattern inlaid. Aggregate may be exposed or recessed. Sand may be strewn over the curing surface to provide a grit finish. Edging or pattern materials such as railroad ties, brick, or wood boards can be used as formwork and left in the slab to produce a very pleasing and decorative element. Since concrete starts out as a thick paste, introducing coloring agents into the mix before it cures will produce very subtle color blends.

Concrete has the advantage of flexibility; it can be cast in a variety of shapes and forms. It is readily available in a pre-mixed or dry form, is moderately inexpensive and easy to form, and provides a workable surface in less than a week. However, concrete does have disadvantages. Due to its porosity, it stains easily and in some cases permanently. Due to its compressive strength, concrete is a very hard material underfoot and produces a hard, nonresilient surface. It absorbs heat during the summer and cold during the winter. In regions of the country where frost penetrates the ground even a few inches, concrete slabs are subject to pitching and heaving. If a heavy rain follows a severe winter, a concrete patio could create flooding problems in the basement. If frost heaving or settling in soft soils is especially severe, a concrete patio will crack, becoming more damaged each season. If it is improperly constructed or reinforced, the concrete will crack as well. These cracks are impossible to repair properly or to remove without replacing the entire section. Contacting your local concrete supplier will give you an idea of the type of material available, special-order information, and the minimum order for on-site delivery.

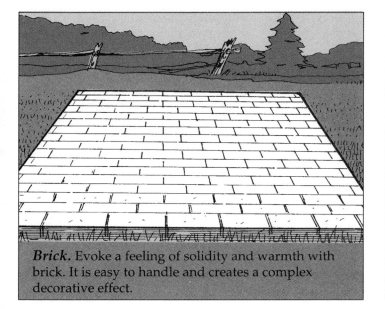

Brick. Evoke a feeling of solidity and warmth with brick. It is easy to handle and creates a complex decorative effect.

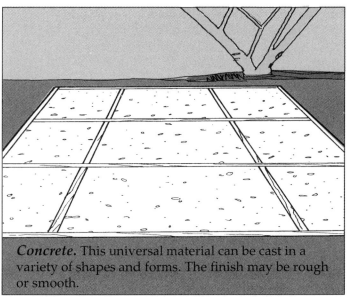

Concrete. This universal material can be cast in a variety of shapes and forms. The finish may be rough or smooth.

Concrete Patio Blocks

Patio blocks are becoming more popular because they come in a variety of colors, shapes and sizes and are an inexpensive surfacing material. An individual unit of concrete block is easily replaced if stained or broken. Concrete block is adaptable for use with a range of edging materials. It is an effective patio or walk choice in combination with railroad ties, brick, cobblestones, or wood board.

Patio block is available at most home centers, lumberyards or concrete suppliers. Construction is similar to that for brick, although the blocks tend to be heavier and larger than brick.

In warmer climates patio blocks are laid into a sand-setting bed. In Northern climates, where freezing and thawing are severe, a concrete setting bed will minimize frost heave.

Concrete Paver Blocks

Interlocking pavers are available in a wide variety of shapes, such as double-hex units, curvilinear units, and other patterns. All interlock or interconnect naturally because of their shape. They require the same installation techniques as regular concrete patio blocks.

Stone

Flagstone, being a natural material, looks good in nearly any setting. It is particularly suited to a garden patio with a rustic atmosphere. Its highly irregular shape and color are an advantage where visual texture is desired.

One disadvantage of using flagstone is that it fractures quite easily if improperly laid. The problem can be solved by placing the stone in a mortar setting bed. Also, be sure to purchase flagstone that has the highest degree of hardness. The harder the flagstone, the longer and more permanent the wearing surface will be.

Cobblestone has a long history as a paving material. They are irregular and difficult to walk on (it is nearly impossible to walk on cobblestone in high heels). In addition, this surface does not drain as well as a smoother one and cobblestone can be slippery after a rain. It also is an awkward supporting surface for tables and chairs.

In a warm climate stone may be laid in a simple sand bed. In a Northern climate, place the stone in a mortar setting bed.

Wood

Pressure-treating techniques have made wood a durable, versatile, relatively cheap and easy-to-install pavement. It may be installed below ground, on grade, or raised to allow the existing drainage to remain essentially unaltered.

Although wood is almost always thought of as a deck material, a patio or walk made of wood is an excellent alternative. Railroad ties and sliced tree trunks offer the potential for a variety of patterns.

Wood is an especially pleasing material for home use. The scale, color, texture, feel—and even the sound it makes when you walk over it—are pleasing and comfortable.

Asphalt

Although seldom considered a decorative material, asphalt combined with other materials can create an attractive and functional patio or walk. The surface may be slippery when wet, but good drainage can take care of this problem. It does require permanent edgings and regular maintenance.

Loose Paving

Gravel is one of the least expensive patio and walk materials. It is available in a variety of sizes and colors. There are two types: peastone gravel, which is a natural rounded gravel, and a man-made gravel such as crushed marble or rock.

Gravel combines well with wood or concrete edging. It can be placed and shaped into a variety of forms and textures that are visually interesting and natural. A gravel patio area is often considered best when used for informal needs since it is difficult to walk on.

When used as a patio, gravel requires raking almost daily. Gravel is a loose material; it scatters easily and tends to wash away in heavy rainfall zones. Gravel also may settle into the ground and will require occasional replenishment.

Bark, wood chips and mulch are excellent materials to use in children's play areas—around swings, slides, etc.—or for woodland walks and patios. It will last as long as three years with a little maintenance, but it will need regular replenishment and permanent edging.

Design Checklist

Shape. Determine which forms and shapes are compatible with the outdoor space. Select a familiar shape such as a square, rectangle, triangle, hexagon or circle. From the physical features of your existing outdoor space you should be able to determine which of those geometric forms would best fit. Use the dominant geometry as the base, then integrate other shapes around the main form. For example, if your outdoor space is predominately rectangular, use a rectangle as the basic form. Then break up the rectangle by using smaller shapes such as squares, triangles or smaller rectangles. Keep in mind that you are designing a space in which people will walk. Try to be as simple as possible while offering enough space for various activities.

Access. Considerations should be made regarding access from the house, as well as from various points on the site. Determine if fencing or walls are required. If so, where and how much will be needed?

Flush with House or Freestanding. A more formal space arrangement is usually enhanced by a freestanding patio, whereas a patio that is built flush to the side of the house creates an informal arrangement. Plan your space to enable different furniture layouts rather than just one.

Landscaping. Building a patio will necessitate an additional amount of landscaping. On the plan of your patio, locate the relative position and types of flowers, plants and shrubs you would like to use. Indicate which ones are new material. If your patio is flush with the house, determine whether or not you plan to locate any

landscaping material next to the wall. Patios often are built at a distance away from the home's foundation so that a line of plants can conceal an unsightly foundation.

Decorative Elements. You may want to incorporate flower boxes, ornamental and reflecting pools, outdoor fireplaces, railings, stairs and tree tubs or openings. You will need visual samples or technical information for each one desired. Try to integrate them into the geometry of the outdoor area, keeping it as simple as possible.

Patterns. Choose the types of paving or patio patterns that are most appropriate to your needs. Not only will different patterns require specific methods of material assembly, but a pattern that fits into the overall geometric scheme will make construction easier.

Design Checklist. Be sure to include all of the details that will make up your patio and the surrounding yard in the final design.

DEVELOPING A SITE PLAN

The first step in building a patio is to develop a site plan. A detailed drawing of the patio design is necessary in order to obtain a building permit. It also will help when estimating the quantities of materials that you will need.

Design the Site

You need to create a measured drawing of the site, along with the patio and its relative position with respect to the lot lines, underground utilities, the water supply and so on. The procedure is quite simple, but it requires a methodical and consistent approach to recording what you see.

You will need to buy some 8¹/₂x11 inches (or larger) grid paper. The grid is normally a light blue printed on a white background. Also, purchase a yardstick or 12-foot measuring tape in order to measure the positions of the various trees, foundations and other structural features. Once you have the grid paper, put it on a clipboard or similar writing platform so the paper will stay in place. At this point you are ready to start working out your site plan.

■ Mark, in the upper corner of the page, the north arrow as well as east, west and south. Then locate the direction from which the prevailing summer and winter winds are likely to come.

■ Select an outside corner of your house at the foundation line. This will become the reference point for all subsequent measurements. From that corner, consistently measure in one direction, either clockwise or counterclockwise.

■ Establish a drawing scale. To do this, give each individual grid a scale value of: 1/4 foot, 1/2 foot, 1 foot, or 2 feet. For example, if you measured 10 feet 6 inches along the foundation wall, this would convert to 21 grid boxes if the scale were "1 grid = 1/2 foot."

■ Measure the entire foundation and mark it onto the grid. Note the northern, southern, eastern and western exposures.

■ Locate the interior room or rooms that will connect to the patio. The procedure is similar to that used to measure and record the foundation. Use the original reference point (corner), measuring around the outside of the house until you arrive at an exterior window or a juncture that also is within the interior space. Locate that point on the interior wall and show it on your plan. Then measure and record the room dimensions at the same scale.

■ Use the information gathered from the local utilities to locate the relative positions of all the pipes and wires. You can then see if there will be any conflict with underground or overhead utilities.

■ Once again, from the reference corner, locate the boundaries or corners of your property. You may find that you will have to attach several pieces of grid paper together to cover your entire lot to scale. Be sure to include the lot lines. This is important in order to meet the zoning setback requirements.

■ Mark the positions of all trees, evergreens and shrubs in the area; noting which will be kept and which will have to be relocated. This will help estimate the amount of work involved. It also will indicate shady areas.

■ Next, add the size and shape of the patio. It is a good idea to make several copies of the original drawing so that you can try more than one design alternative. It is important that you compare several plan arrangements. This allows you to experiment with size and shape possibilities and to begin to estimate quantities and types of materials.

■ Once you have decided upon a design, draw up the plan at a larger scale. This drawing will be limited to the area immediately around the patio and the house as well as any trees, evergreens, flower beds or shrubs. The larger-scale plan will help you visualize the patterns and textures of your materials and will give you a more accurate feeling for the relative size. To accomplish this, simply convert the previous measurements to another scale. For example, if you measured 10 feet, 6 inches, along the foundation wall, this would convert to 63 grid boxes with a scale of 1 grid box = 2 inches, or to 42 grid boxes if the scale were 1 grid box = 3 inches.

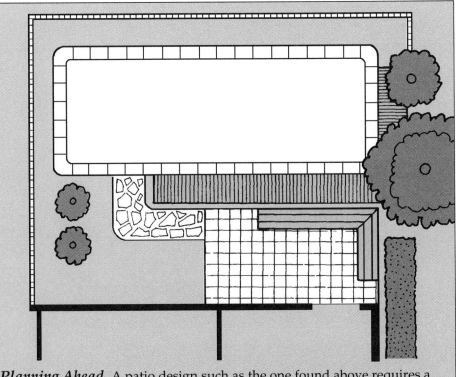

Planning Ahead. A patio design such as the one found above requires a great deal of planning. To plan your patio, no matter what the style, follow the instructions found on the following page.

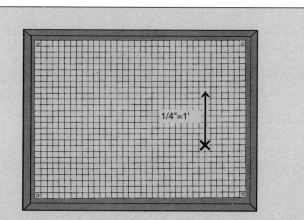

1 Use a large sheet of grid paper. Decide what scale you will use; 1/4 in. on the paper equaling 1 ft. on the ground is standard. X marks the house corner where measuring starts.

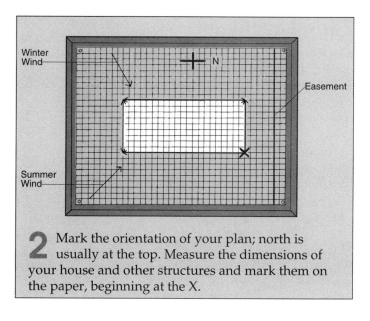

2 Mark the orientation of your plan; north is usually at the top. Measure the dimensions of your house and other structures and mark them on the paper, beginning at the X.

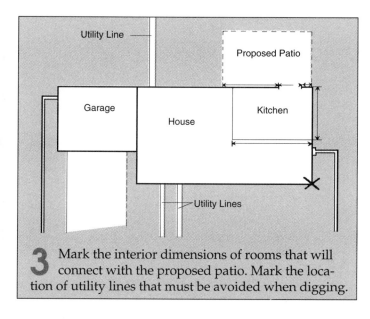

3 Mark the interior dimensions of rooms that will connect with the proposed patio. Mark the location of utility lines that must be avoided when digging.

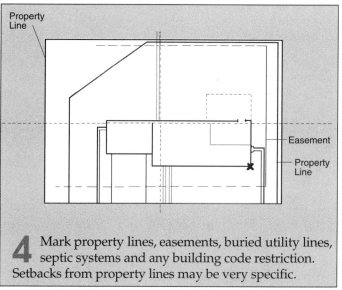

4 Mark property lines, easements, buried utility lines, septic systems and any building code restriction. Setbacks from property lines may be very specific.

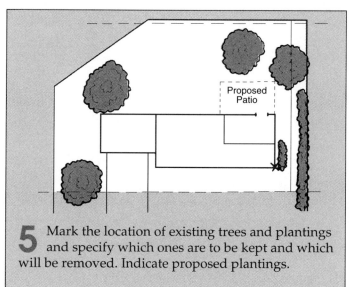

5 Mark the location of existing trees and plantings and specify which ones are to be kept and which will be removed. Indicate proposed plantings.

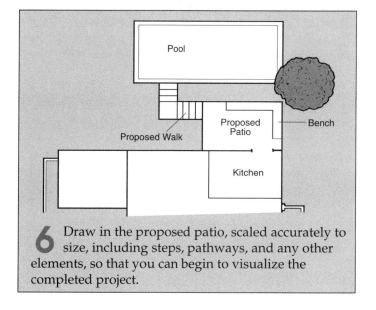

6 Draw in the proposed patio, scaled accurately to size, including steps, pathways, and any other elements, so that you can begin to visualize the completed project.

Patio Layout

You are now ready to lay out the site for your patio. Proper layout of the patio area is necessary before you can accurately estimate quantities of materials and acquire a building permit. It also reduces the difficulties of construction. By following the steps given earlier you should have already measured the exterior space and have all obstacles and utilities marked.

■ In laying out the patio, locate all trees, bushes, shrubs and plants that are to be kept within the patio zone. Make sure you have indicated all plantings adjacent to the patio. Prior to construction, you will want to protect them from damage as you build the patio.

■ If you desire outdoor lighting, locate approximately where those lines must go. Once the patio is down, it is quite expensive and time-consuming to rip it up and install a line or pipe.

■ At this point, you should be able to clearly indicate the depth and breadth of your patio and the material selected. Determine the exact size and location with respect to the foundation of your house or building.

■ Determine how far the site slopes within the area. This will help in setting the level of the patio surface. Plot out carefully the edges or borders. If they are to be a specific material, you should indicate their size.

■ If your design is to include any screens, walls, fences or trellises, you should locate their position relative to the patio.

■ If building an overhead cover, it is necessary to build the framing structure before the patio is built. This is because the patio would interfere with the support posts. Decide now how the materials are to be transported and erected. In most cases the patio surface can be altered to accommodate the structures to be placed over or near it.

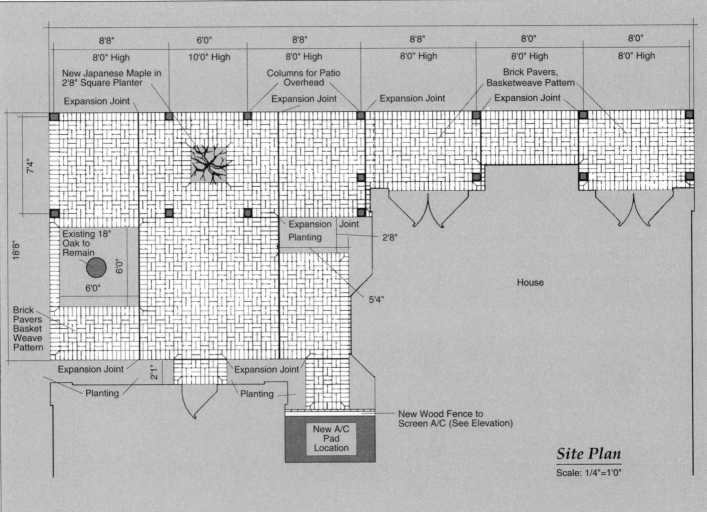

Detailed Site Plan. Creating a site plan reduces the difficulties of construction. It also helps when estimating quantities of materials and acquiring a building permit.

GRADING & DRAINAGE

Drainage affects walks, walls, fences, patios, retaining walls—anything that lays on the earth or penetrates it, including plants. Before changing anything in your yard, it is important that you understand all the variables involved in good drainage. Most people think of good drainage only as shaping a lawn so that rain water runs off to the street and gutters and disappears. That is part of drainage, but not all of it.

The Ground

In order to study drainage, you need to know at least a little about soil.

The Earth is made up of many types of soil. The ground can vary a great deal in a very short distance. For example, your house may be built on clay or rock strata while a neighbor down the street may have a house that is built on sandy soil. Rain soaks into these different soils at different rates, depending on how loose or compact they are. Clays are tight, fine-grained soils; sandy soils are loose. The differences between these nearly opposite soil types is something like the difference between coffee grinds. Water runs through a coarse, loosely packed grind quicker than through a fine, tightly packed grind. Anyone who has ever made drip coffee knows this. Therefore, drainage is not just directing water off the surface, it also involves the ability of the soil to let water soak down through it.

Plants. During the different seasons the amount of rainfall will vary as will, of course, the temperature. Plants, left to natural methods of procreation and travel, will go where they need to go—where the soil, water, and temperature suit them. Unless you are willing to import soil to match the needs of the plant, (trees are plants as well) select plants that flourish naturally in your area. This kind of importing will work with small plants more easily than with trees because of their deep root systems. This is not to say you should not tamper with nature (as a purist might say). However, your landscaping will work better if you know enough about soil to match the plants to the soil. Avoid fad plants sold to create exotic effects.

Water. Drainage affects all our structures, especially in extreme cold. Water expands when it freezes. You must take care to keep water from building up under walks, other paving, foundations, along the earth side of retaining walls and so forth. The general rule is to keep the ground under structures as dry as possible. The obvious part of drainage, surface drainage, can be handled by assuring that you always grade so that water runs away from your structures and is not allowed to build up around them.

One of the simplest ways to accomplish this is to create a swale (a simple, shallow depression). This will guide water that otherwise would not be shed away from the surface structure. If the arrangement of structures on your lot has created a depression, it may be necessary to construct a catch basin to collect the water and an underground line to carry off the water. Avoid this solution, if possible, because it is difficult and expensive. Catch basins and drainage lines usually require planning by an engineer or architect.

In addition, underground drainage is usually controlled by using materials that drain well. You protect walks, paving, floor slabs, foundation footings and other elements in contact with the earth by laying a bed of gravel or sand underneath them. Assuming the surface drainage is adequate, the gravel or sand directs water away and keeps the structures from being damaged by freezing water. Retaining walls and other vertical surfaces can be protected by laying a vertical bed of gravel up along them and by providing drainage weep holes to allow water to escape through them. Drainage standards are available from your community building department for nearly any structure you might build either above or below ground.

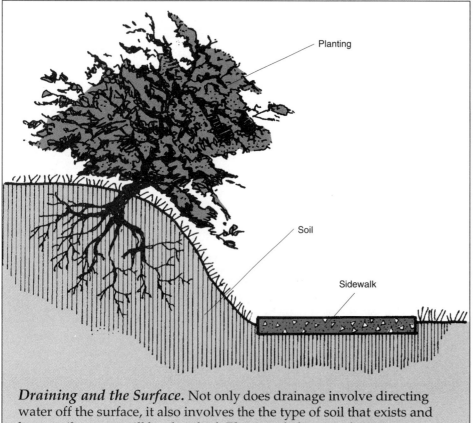

Draining and the Surface. Not only does drainage involve directing water off the surface, it also involves the the type of soil that exists and how easily water will be absorbed. Plantings help control erosion.

Planting

Soil

Sidewalk

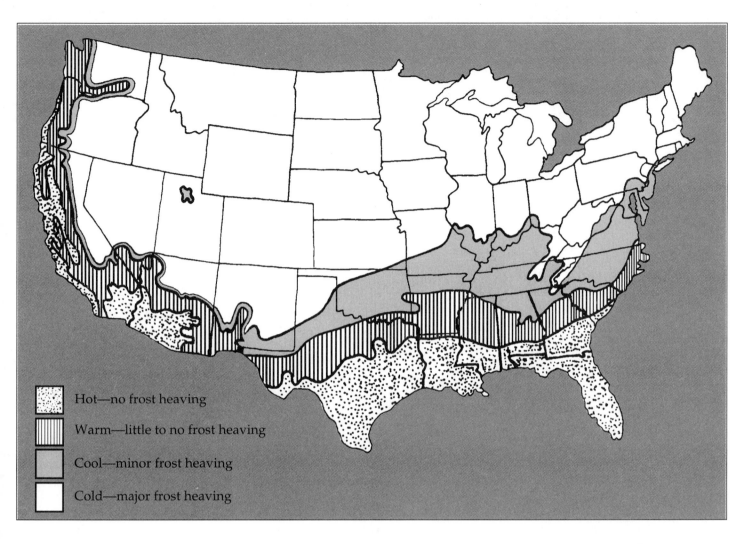

Hot—no frost heaving

Warm—little to no frost heaving

Cool—minor frost heaving

Cold—major frost heaving

Frost Heave. Cold weather creates special problems for most structures—especially for those built on clay soil. Water that freezes in any soil will cause it to expand, often moving or damaging structures within the soil, but clay soils are the worst. For example, in a very cold region, a fence post that was dropped into moist spring clay, may be squirted out the following January. This natural process is called frost heave.

There is no cure for frost heave, but there are a few ways to minimize its effects:

■ Improve drainage beneath and around underground structural elements so that water cannot build up. This is accomplished with sand or gravel. By modifying (removing) some of the clay soil that is next to the underground element, you improve the drainage. At times it is necessary to use this method in a wholesale manner. For example, the clay soil under a building slab might be removed completely down to the frost line (the frost line is the depth to which the earth freezes) and replaced with a soil that is less susceptible to frost heave. However, this solution may be impractical in some areas where the frost line may be almost as deep as the above-ground height of the building or wall.

■ Another way of protecting structures beneath the ground is to extend the footings beneath the frost line. This method can be expensive in areas of extreme cold.

For protection against frost heave in areas where it is a serious problem, you need to consult either a local civil engineer or your building department for advice pertaining to your particular project.

Drainage is a complicated issue. Professionals, laymen, and others associated with building and landscaping have developed standards for building and planting in all parts of the country. Often a phone call to the right person (your building department or agricultural extension service is often the place to start) can give you all the information you need in a few minutes. Usually, they will assist you without assessing a fee.

Grading Your Lot

As indicated earlier, most of us inherited the soil and drainage accommodations the developer left with us. Although the grading was done to efficiently get the water off each lot and to some disposal point, it probably was accomplished the cheapest way possible. This usually means no retaining walls or catch basins (drainage devices that allow you more freedom to create interesting and useful spaces like terraces, walks and walls) were used.

This is not meant to be a criticism. A developer of speculative housing is required to provide drainage so that each house is protected from flooding. To do more (by spending money on custom landscaping) is asking him to gamble his investment on what an unknown buyer might want. However, in new developments it is not uncommon for a developer to extract his landscaping allowance and give it directly to the purchaser. Then, the new owner may contract separately for the landscaping plan he would like. The developer may prefer to modify the plan to suit the buyer.

Grading Theory

To understand basic grading, it might help to think of your rough lot as an aluminum foil pie pan. Assume the pan is dented and warped. If you place a small quantity of water at one side, and then tilt the pan, the water will take a certain course around the warps and into the dents. Some of the water reaches the other side and some remains in the dents. If you level the dents and straighten out the warps, you can influence the way the water reaches the other side.

If you add a child's building block as representative of your house, you can reshape the surface of the pan so that the water runs around the block to the other side of the pan without touching the block. But, by adding a block representing a garage or a children's play area, you run into conflicts. When you get the water away from the house, you notice it runs against the garage. Clear that problem and perhaps the play area stands in water.

The cheapest way to handle surface drainage like this is to manipulate the surface of the lot until water runs to the street without disturbing any of the structures, including walks and patios.

Making Changes

When you begin to make changes to your lot—by adding patios, drives, walks, walls, steps, raised flower beds or gardens—you need to study the existing drainage pattern. This can be done easily by observing a heavy rain. (The heavier the rain the better.) If you are adding only an item or two—one patio and a walk, for example—and you think that is all you will be adding, you should conform to existing drainage patterns as much as possible. If, however, you know that over the years you will be altering your lawn radically, it is better to plan the whole development in advance and then add the new elements in accordance with the total plan. You may need a landscape architect for this.

Often the drainage pattern you inherited is far from adequate for the landscaping plan you have in mind. If this is the case, utilize some of the landscaping aids found in this book, such as, retaining walls of varying height, material and design; steps of all kinds; dry wells; walls, walks and fences. Retaining walls allow you to raise or lower areas. Steps allow you to move from one level to another comfortably. Dry wells may keep trouble spots dry. Walls and fences can offer privacy, security, a wind break and a degree of noise protection. They also may cut down on direct sunlight. Walks protect your feet and guide visitors through your outdoor living spaces. All of these elements can be beautiful as well as functional. They also require attention to drainage.

While your goals in landscaping may be purely aesthetic—to create a beautiful setting to live and relax in— it is difficult to separate beauty from function. Do not try to force a physical form on your lawn that it was not meant to have. For example, an almost perfectly flat lawn in Kansas is not likely to be enhanced by building unnatural earth terraces, retaining walls, or other unexpected structures.

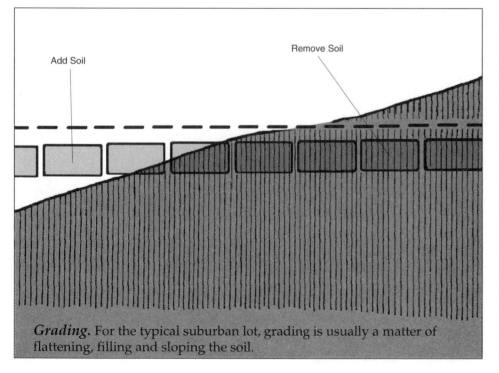

Grading. For the typical suburban lot, grading is usually a matter of flattening, filling and sloping the soil.

Grading Practice

If you are not making extreme changes, you can do most residential grading with a few hand tools, some stakes, and a line level. Grading, for the typical suburban lot, is usually a matter of flattening, smoothing and sloping the soil to drain away from the house and other structures to lower disposal points. If you have an uneven lot and you want a variety of space uses on it, the planning and execution may give you some trouble. A good grading plan will divert water away from your house and all your projects in a functional and aesthetically pleasing manner without drainage conflicts between the different areas. This can be rather complicated to work out on paper. You may need a landscape architect to help you recognize and plan the contours, but you can still do the project yourself.

Reshaping the Ground Slope. In an undeveloped lot, you would want to slope your front yard to drain toward the street.

■ First loosen the soil with a double-ended pick (a pick at one end and a blade at the other). You then can use a long-handled, pointed shovel to fill the obvious depressions and level any mounds. If it is necessary to use a wheelbarrow to move the dirt, rent one with a pneumatic tire and sturdy framing. Work with the lot until it looks flat. Next use a rotary tiller and break up the soil until the clods are a convenient size for raking with a garden rake. Till back and forth in a tight grid pattern. Then rake the lot as smooth as you can with the rake.

■ Now you are ready to determine the existing slope and plan your new one. Following the example below, place a stake at one corner of the foundation wall of your house. Place another stake at the edge of the sidewalk, aligned and even with the first stake. Attach a string to the foundation wall stake at a point at least 8 inches down from the level of the first floor inside. Stretch the string to the stake at the sidewalk and attach it, leveling it with a line level. Make sure the string is not touching the ground anywhere. If it is, dig a trench under the string so it does not touch the ground. Measure up from the sidewalk to the string, and you will have the vertical rise. Measure the distance between the stakes, and you will have the horizontal run. Repeat this staking process at the opposite corner of the house.

■ To figure the slope, divide the inches of rise by the inches of run. The result will be the degree (percentage of) slope. For example, if the difference between the house and sidewalk is 5 inches and the distance from the house is 20 feet (240 inches), the slope is 2%.

■ Stretch a line between the stakes at the sidewalk edge and attach where the first strings are tied. Now you have described a string boundary around the lot to be sloped. Drive stakes at 6-foot intervals around the string boundary and connect them with strings, forming a string gridwork over the lot. Check the strings for level with a line level.

■ Now you can move around the lot within the grid, shoveling and raking the soil so that it slopes down to the sidewalk at the desired rate. The string grid provides you with a handy slope check at many points on the lot. Use a yardstick regularly to check the distance between the string and the soil.

■ Repeat the process around the house, establishing the grade you want on each side. The rate of the slope away from the house, the drive and the different use areas varies according to the particular lay of your lot.

■ When you have graded the soil as you want it, tamp it lightly to minimize uneven settlement.

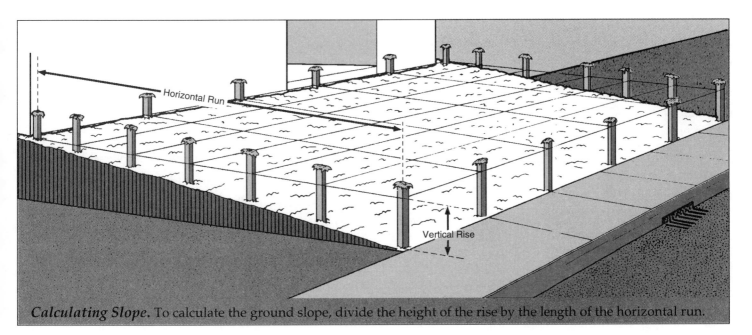

Calculating Slope. To calculate the ground slope, divide the height of the rise by the length of the horizontal run.

Erosion Control

Sloping the lot away from the house, as described on page 25, is one of the typical methods of surface drainage. The purpose of such drainage is to protect some object, such as the house, or to keep areas from standing in water. On lots where there are steep natural grades, you must take steps to prevent erosion. You probably will want to choose the cheapest and simplest method.

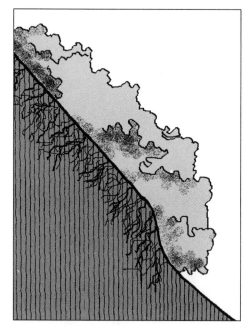

Groundcovers

Erosion can be controlled by slowing down the runoff of surface water. Often you can do this by simply planting groundcover. Sandwort, Thrift, Dianthus, Juniper, Pachysandra, and Taxus are good groundcovers that will prosper in many parts of the country. These covers grow thickly, squeezing out most weeds and becoming a neat, uniform cover.

However, groundcovers alone may not be enough for some steep slopes. You may have to modify the slope itself, mixing groundcovers with stones, baffles, swales and terraces to slow down the flow of water over the slope.

Stones

One of the easiest ways to stop erosion on steep slopes is with stones. All you have to do is line the slope with stones large enough to stay in place when water runs over them. Most stones have one flat side, so laying them is usually not a problem. Use a pointed shovel to scoop out enough earth so that the stones are in a secure position. The number and sizes of stone you use depends on the steepness of the slope and the amount of water that will run over it. A 4- to 6-inch layer of stones set approximately 2 inches or more in the ground should take care of most problem situations. You may want the entire surface covered with stone; however, you could space the stones somewhat and plant a ground cover between them. This will soften the appearance of the slope. A ground cover and stone combination is an attractive solution to the problem of erosion.

Baffles

A baffle is any structure that will slow the flow of surface water by slight diversion. A baffle may be built of pressure-treated wood cross ties, stone, masonry—or some combination of these materials. To use a cross tie baffle, lay the tie on the slope perpendicular to the flow of water. Deciding how deep to secure the tie in the earth is a matter of judgment; usually burying the tie halfway should be enough. If the ties are unsightly, you may want to bury them a little deeper, but remember, their purpose is to slow water.

How many baffles are needed is another matter of judgment that depends on the steepness of the slope and the amount of water that flows over it. You can experiment with a few cross ties and add more after you observe the water action during a rain.

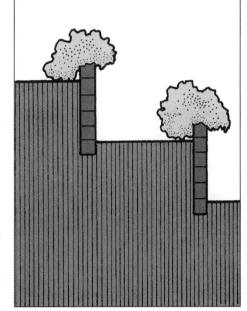

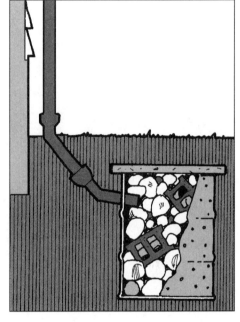

Swales

Swales, ground depressions, will help you deal with water on steep slopes. The size and number of swales you need depend—as do all the other solutions—on the steepness of the slope and the amount of water that comes over it. For example, a mild slope might be handled by digging a swale 2 inches deep and about 18 inches wide. Round off the edges. Take the dirt you scoop out and lay it along the down side of the swale, patting it with the shovel to form a lip. This helps keep the water from running over the swale. The swales should be laid almost perpendicular to the direction of the water flow so that the water runs along the swale in the direction you choose.

Retaining Walls

Another way to slow down surface water on steep slopes is to build retaining wall terraces. Generally, what retaining walls do is separate an area into terraces that can be drained more easily than one large area. A series of retaining walls will control both drainage and erosion problems. Retaining wall construction varies widely in expense and difficulty. Railroad ties are durable and frequently used. Most walls require weep holes to relieve the buildup of water behind the wall.

You create terraces by digging and manipulating the surface. Unless you have problem soil, a pick, pointed shovel, garden rake and wheelbarrow are the only tools you will need. The terraces resemble a set of giant steps. These steps, when reinforced by retaining walls and planted with grass or a ground cover, should slow down the flow of the surface water.

Dry Wells

In some cases, it is difficult or impossible to grade for drainage economically. An example of this occurs when several natural swales are formed by two or more planes of land coming together. As a result, a low spot is formed. In this case, you may be able to eliminate the standing water by digging a dry well.

A dry well is simply a pit filled with coarse gravel or masonry rubble that allows water to run down through it quickly. The size of the dry well depends on the amount of water that it will have to absorb and on the depth of the water table. The building department can tell you how deep the water table is in your area. It is advisable to have an engineer or your building inspector check your plan before you begin work. The bottom of the well must be above the seasonal height of the water table.

Points to Remember

The first consideration in drainage is to keep the house—and the access routes to it—safe from flooding or excessive water. To accomplish this, a protective slope is draped around the house like an apron; protective swales may be used in combination with the slopes. The design of these protective measures varies with your particular lot. If you do not use a landscape architect for planning your contours, have the building department check your plans.

Protect Your Property

Avoid grades that allow water to reach the foundation walls of new buildings or become trapped against new garden walls. This water can seep into basements and crawl spaces and cause mildew problems. A water buildup also exerts a great deal of pressure that can crack and weaken foundations of both houses and walls.

Respect Neighbor's Property

When planning or executing grading for drainage, study the grading of the houses on each side of your house and behind it. You can end up in a law suit if you divert runoff onto a neighbor's property. If a new house is built on a vacant lot next to you and causes you a drainage problem, call your building department. This is not unfriendly to your new neighbor; the building department can tell what the problem is and isolate responsibility quickly. In typical subdivision layout, all drainage patterns may lead to the street, draining from a ridge located along the back property lines of adjoining lots of all the houses. Perhaps part of the water may go to a swale along the back property lines, or a combination of these two, or more drainage plans may be used. In other words, your property is part of an overall drainage plan. It is your responsibility to make any changes in your drainage plan fit the overall plan and not disturb it or your neighbors. Extensive changes in drainage often require consultation with a landscape architect or civil engineer.

Slope new paving toward existing drainage aids such as swales, ditches, catch basins and dry wells.

Climate Extremes

In areas subject to frost heave, drainage becomes more critical because buildings, walls, paving and fencing can be damaged or destroyed by it. If you live in an area that gets extremely cold, check with an architect or your building department for specific advice on drainage for projects you have in mind and for drainage problems you may be experiencing with a finished lot (see page 23).

Prevent Excess Erosion

Sharp corners erode more quickly than smooth ones. Round off the edges of swales you dig with a shovel. Take the earth you removed for the swale and form a lip, or slight berm, at the lower edge of the swale. Pat the berm smooth and compact with your shovel.

Drainage ditches and swales often run almost perpendicular to the flow of water down slopes they help drain. This way, they catch the most water and change its direction. Sometimes it is necessary to run swales or ditches in the direction of the water flow. When this is the case, line the bottom of the swale with stone or rubble (set deep enough so the water does not pull it out) to prevent erosion of the swale or ditch. A pointed shovel is all you need to set the stones or rubble into place.

Add Catch Basins or Dry Wells

When catch basins must be used, they should be installed where they will never overflow toward the house if they should become stopped up and overflow. The overall drainage and grading plan should be contoured so that if the basin should overflow, any water would flow away from the house.

If you use a dry well to drain problem areas, check with the building department to determine the depth of the ground water table. The bottom of the dry well should be above the water table at its seasonal height. Keep dry wells as far as possible from buildings and foundations of other structures. It should also be noted that the bottom of the dry well must project into a strata of porous soil capable of absorbing the water from the well. If you are unsure about the character of your subsoil, check with local experts such as a landscape architect, civil engineer, the building department or HUD, before proceeding with this project.

Protect Utilities

Check with the utility and phone companies for location of existing underground lines before you dig. In addition, install any underground lines or equipment you may want before you begin paving.

Finally, it must be said that in dealing with the problems of drainage and grading, it is impossible to cover all possible situations. No one can give anything but example solutions to typical problems.

WORKING WITH CONCRETE

Although concrete work is predictable and easily learned by most do-it-yourselfers, there are a few precautions to be taken. Handling concrete is back-breaking work, so do not overdo it, especially the first day or two. Since concrete is so heavy, forms must be strong enough to hold the semi-liquid material in place until it sets up. If this aspect is neglected, you can end up with a broken form and a yard full of expensive concrete, not to mention possible injury.

Concrete Tools

Tools for Preparation

Shovels and hoes are necessary for moving the material around in the forms, as well as a garden hose and water supply for cleaning tools. You also should have a pair of rubber hip boots for wading around in the material. Sooner or later you are going to have to get right in the "mud." Always be careful not to let your skin come in contact with wet cement as it can cause skin burns.

Wheelbarrow and Mortar Box. You will need a wheelbarrow to move the material to the form. A small garden wheelbarrow is not good enough; you will need a large, sturdy contractor's wheelbarrow, preferably one that has wooden handles and a large pneumatic tire. If you mix the material yourself and plan on mixing only small batches, you can perform the task in a wheelbarrow, a special mixing tub or on a flat, level surface such as a driveway. Another option is a mortar box. These boxes come in several different sizes, the smaller ranging from an 11x23x42 inches box that holds 6 cubic feet of material to one that is 11x35x82 inches and holds 15 cubic feet. For hand mixing, you will need a mortar hoe.

Power Mixers. A much faster method is to utilize a power mixer, which will be required if you are adding an air-entraining agent. (An air-entraining admixture is mandatory in areas with severe winters and frost heave.) Mixers come in a range of sizes, from a small 1½ cubic feet wheelbarrow size that can be rolled to the job to a large 6 cubic feet mixer that is pulled behind an automobile. You can rent mixers from most tool rental yards in larger cities. Most mixers come equipped with an electric motor or a gas motor (used in more remote locations). Incidentally, if you rent a gasoline-powered unit, make sure you have the rental people start the motor to see that it operates easily.

Tools for Placing

You should use a special concrete hoe or a square-ended shovel for placing the concrete in the forms. Use a concrete rake for tamping down small jobs and a vibrator for very large jobs. (Do not use ordinary garden tools when you work with concrete—they can separate the water from the rest of the mixture and ruin the project.) You also will need 2x4 boards to use as screeds or strikeboards. These pull the excess concrete off the forms. The boards should be straight and lightweight and should measure about 1 to 3 feet longer than the width of the form.

Tools for Finishing

You will need several tools for finishing concrete. These include floats and darbies, which you can purchase or make out of wood. Floats provide an even but fairly rough finish. The final smooth finish is applied with metal trowels—several different kinds are available. You also will need an edger for finishing the edges of walks and patios, as well as a groover for cutting the control joints. The blade on the groover must be 1 inch deep (or 1/4 of the thickness of the slab). If you need to trowel a large area, you can rent a power trowel. Broomed finishes require the use of a stiff-bristled shop broom or a special concrete broom, which you can buy.

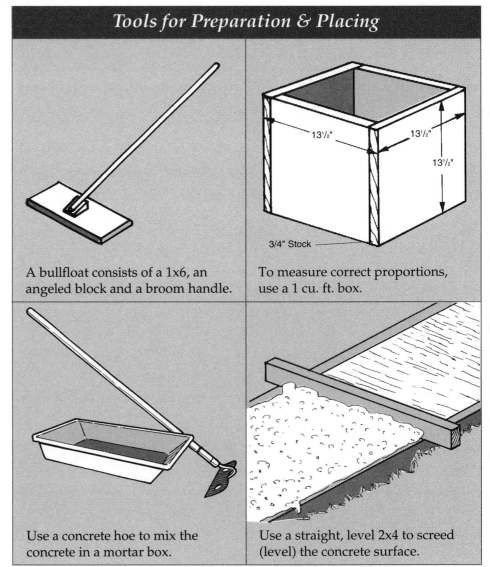

Tools for Preparation & Placing

A bullfloat consists of a 1x6, an angeled block and a broom handle.

To measure correct proportions, use a 1 cu. ft. box.

Use a concrete hoe to mix the concrete in a mortar box.

Use a straight, level 2x4 to screed (level) the concrete surface.

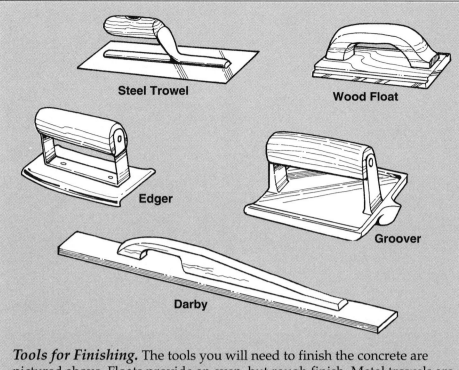

Tools for Finishing. The tools you will need to finish the concrete are pictured above. Floats provide an even, but rough finish. Metal trowels are used to create a smooth surface. Edgers are used to create neat edges.

Type I. This general purpose cement is commonly used in residential work.

Type II. This cement is used for bridges and pilings. It provides some sulfate resistance and moderate hydration heat.

Type III. This cement hardens more quickly than Types I and II, generating more heat in the process. It is most commonly used on commercial structures such as smoke stacks, in which the forms are moved as quickly as the material sets up. It also is used for work done in the winter and rush jobs.

Type IV. Used for massive structures, this cement produces less heat than the others

Type V. This cement offers high sulfate resistance and is used in areas that have a high sulfate content in the water and/or soil.

Aggregates

Aggregate, the second material used in concrete, ranges in size from tiny dust particles of sand to 2 1/2-inch stones used as larger "fill." Ideally, aggregate combines both small-and large particles to make the strongest concrete. The small pieces fill in around the larger pieces. For most home masonry, the aggregates used are sand and gravel.

Sand. "Bank-run" sand is best, due to its rounded, various-sized particles. The sand size can run up to as large as 1/4 inch in diameter. Do not use something called "sharp sand," which is used for mortar.

Gravel. The stones may be as large as 1 in. They can be screened for uniform size, or they can be bank run, which also may include some coarse sand along with the gravel.

Naturally, the larger the aggregates, the more economical the material will be. The concrete will require less cement and the finished slab will suffer less from shrinkage. However, do not use aggregate larger than 1/4 of the thickness of the pour.

Materials

Concrete is actually a mixture of sand, gravel or other aggregates, and portland cement (this is not a brand name, but a type of concrete) mixed with enough water to form a semi-fluid state. This mixture is then poured into a form to harden.

Cement

Cement is not the same as concrete; cement is one of the ingredients used in concrete. Portland cement is actually a mixture of burned clay, lime, iron, silica and alumina. This mixture is put through a kiln at 2700°F and then ground to a fine powder. Gypsum is then added. Cement is available in gray, white and some shades of buff.

Cement comes packaged in 1 cubic foot bags that weigh 94 pounds. Sacks of cement are quite heavy for their size and are a bit awkward to handle, especially if you have to lift them in and out of a deep car trunk. Take your time and do not strain yourself trying to lift them.

Moisture Absorption and Premature Hardening. One problem with cement is that it absorbs moisture quickly. Once enough water has been absorbed, the cement hardens and is completely useless. Make sure that you check the material purchased at the building supply dealer to see that none of the sacks have already hardened. Some bags may seem to be somewhat hardened around the edges, but if they loosen up after they are rolled around on the floor, they should be alright.

Once you have the cement home, you must store the bags up off the ground; otherwise, they will absorb moisture. They also should not be stored on a concrete floor or slab, as they will take moisture from the concrete. Instead, stack the concrete sacks on wooden skids. Cover the bags with plastic or other waterproof covering if you must store outside.

Types of Cement. There are five basic cement types. The one most used in home masonry work is Type I, which is carried by nearly all building supply yards.

Mixing Concrete

Years ago concrete was mixed entirely by hand. You can do the same, but it will take time and practice before you get used to the job. Concrete mixing is hard work. You can make it easier by pacing yourself instead of rushing. Make sure you have good balance, and use your entire body to mix instead of just your arms. Do not use a shovel to lift materials more often than you have to. Use a mixing hoe instead—a large-bladed hoe with two holes in the blade. When only a shovel can do the job, do not use a shovel that is too large for you to handle comfortably.

1 Choosing a Mixing Site. To hand mix concrete you need a clean, smooth, flat surface. Even a concrete driveway or floor will do—just make sure you hose down and clean up the floor after mixing the material. Usually, though, there are two basic sites for hand mixing—a wheelbarrow (if you have a fairly large one) or a mortar box. This can be rented or purchased—or you can build your own. The mortar box is usually quite a bit larger and easier to use than the wheelbarrow. However, once the concrete is ready, you still have to shovel the material up into the wheelbarrow and move it to the job. This can be an arduous task, so my favorite method is to use a large contractor's wheelbarrow as the mixing site. Whichever you use, mix no more than the container can hold. In fact, if you are using a wheelbarrow, mix only 1 or 2 cubic feet of concrete until you know how to mix properly and can handle the weight of the wheelbarrow.

2 Measuring the Ingredients. Use a bucket to measure the ingredients, leveling off the material with a shovel to produce proper amounts. Place the materials in layers on top of each other, beginning with the gravel, then sand, then cement. Before you add the water, move the wheelbarrow (if you are using one) next to the form you plan to fill—the load will be lighter than after the water is added.

3 Mixing Dry Ingredients. Use a concrete hoe to mix all the dry ingredients before adding water.

4 Adding the Water. Measure a gallon of water so you keep to the proportions you need. Using a mixing hoe, make a shallow depression in the center of the material and pour in a little water. Mix this thoroughly—get clear down into the stones in the bottom of the mix. Then add more water. Pull more dry material in from the sides, and keep mixing it in thoroughly. Any dry materials will weaken the concrete.

Mortar Box Method

Mixing concrete in a mortar box is similar to mixing it in a wheelbarrow, except the materials should be placed in layers in about two-thirds of the box, leaving empty the areas next to the boards. Add a little water in the empty end and rake some of the material into the water. Then mix the two. This process continues until the correct proportions and mix are achieved. All of the dry ingredients can be mixed before adding the water, if preferred. However, mixing the ingredients as they are pulled into the water takes less work.

1 Mix the concrete on a clean, flat surface. A wheelbarrow or mortar box can be used or simply a driveway or piece of plywood.

2 Carefully measure the proper amounts of each ingredient.

3 Mix the dry ingredients thoroughly with a hoe or rake.

4 Make a shallow depression in the center of the dry materials and alternate pouring water and mixing until thoroughly mixed.

Troubleshooting Problems

Too much water, or too little. One problem that you will soon figure out is that the more water is added to the mix, the easier the mix is to work with, and also the easier it is to pour into the forms.

Testing Concrete Mix. When you have mixed the concrete to your satisfaction, you can test to see if it is correct by making the settling test.

The settling test is based on the stiffness of ridges in the concrete. First, smack the concrete with the back of a shovel. Then, jab it lightly with a hoe to make a series of ridges. If the surface is smooth and the grooves maintain their separation, the mix is right. If the ridges slump back down and cannot be seen easily, there is too much water. If you cannot create distinct ridges, there is too little water (see diagrams right).

Poor Mixing. Make sure you have mixed all the ingredients properly and thoroughly, scraping them from the sides and bottom of the wheelbarrow or mixing box. The concrete mix should be an even color. Light or dark streaks indicate poor mixing.

Remedying a Poor Mix. If your mix is too wet, it does not have enough sand and aggregate for the amount of cement paste. Add 5 to 10 percent more of sand and aggregate, mix well, and test. Repeat this until the mix is correct. Keep careful notes of the added amounts; when you make the new batch, you will follow the revised figures for sand and coarse aggregate.

If your mix is too stiff, it has too much aggregate. Do not try to remedy the situation by simply adding water. Instead, add a cement-water solution that has proportions of 2 to 1. Unfortunately, in most cases even this will not work and you will have to start over again with decreased amounts of sand and coarse aggregate. Experiment, keeping track of the decreased proportions, until you have the correct amount of water and ingredients.

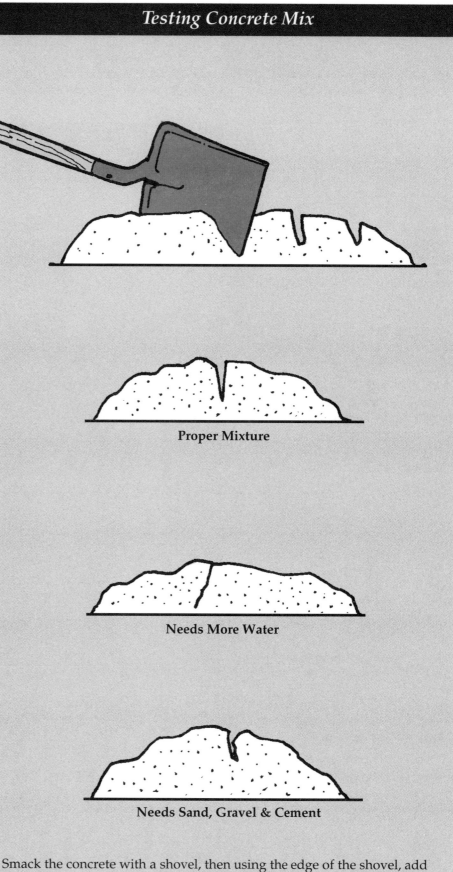

Testing Concrete Mix

Proper Mixture

Needs More Water

Needs Sand, Gravel & Cement

Smack the concrete with a shovel, then using the edge of the shovel, add a series of small ridges. The mix is right if the grooves maintain their separation.

Preparing the Site

Remove all the topsoil and sod within the area designated for the walk or patio. Then, drive several stakes around the perimeter, allowing at least one foot beyond the actual edge of the area.

Rake the ground, removing any large rocks, glass or debris in the excavation area. The depth of the excavation will depend on the thickness of the slab, and whether the walk or patio wearing surface will be aboveground or flush with the ground level.

After you have levelled the site, and while you are excavating, you will have to grade the earth so that a drainage problem will not result (for example, the corners of the patio furthest from the house will be lower than the point closest to it).

Smooth out the surface as much as possible by raking. In many cases, you can grade just by moving the earth from low spots to the desired high areas. Finally, level and tamp the area.

If your site slopes steeply away from or toward the house foundation, try to level and grade it as much as possible. To do this might require additional excavation beyond the depth of the topsoil. It may be necessary to call in a landscape grader if the grade requires much earth fill.

If fill is required, determine the quantity by figuring the height to be achieved over the area to be covered. This figure should then be double as the fill will compact to almost one half of its original volume.

To fill a site, put the greatest amount of soil where the greatest void exists, spread it around, and tamp. The tamping may be done by a large roller or by a mechanical tamper that can be rented.

Continue to infill in 4-inch layers. Keep the soil moist but not wet. The soil will absorb the moisture and swell, which will be its natural state when covered by the concrete slab. To check for the desired level, pick one of the straightest 2x4s. Lay it down over the area placing on it a carpenter's level, on edge. You must find the level before you can create the pitch. This will tell you which areas need more fill or stripping. Check for levelness on the diagonal as well.

Always tamp down thoroughly.

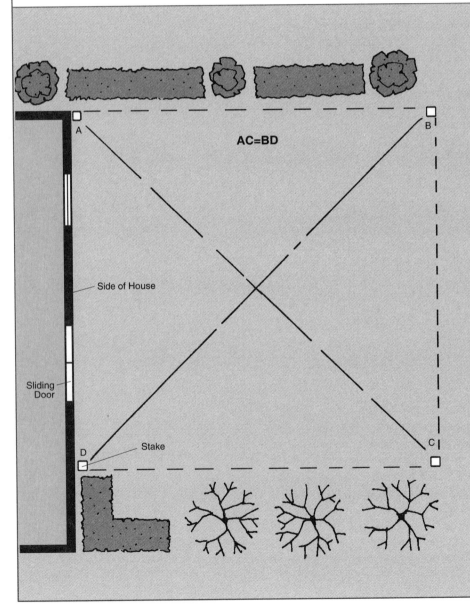

Square Patio

To lay out a square patio, measure the width of the patio and stake out two corners along the house wall. Then measure the desired length from those marks out in the yard. Drive stakes where the two outer corners will fall. Working on the diagonal, measure between opposite corners. The two diagonal distances must be the same. If they are not, shift the outer stakes until the measurements are equal. This assures a square layout. Then run strings between the stakes around the perimeter of the patio.

AC=BD

Side of House

Sliding Door

Stake

1. A patio does not have to be square; it can be designed free form. There are several technical ways to lay out circular and curved edges, but the easiest is to "draw" the outline, right on the lawn, with a regular garden hose. Since a patio usually is quite large, irregularities in curved areas will not be notice-able. Once you like the shape of the area, set tables, chairs and other items inside the boundaries. Walk around the area and adjust the perimeter as you please. When you are satisfied, run a stake-and-string outline that follows the line of the hose.

2. Pour sand or lime over the mason's line, transferring the outline of the patio to the ground. Then, carefully remove the stake-and-string outline.

3. Prepare to pour the sand bed and the slab. Remove all vegetation and excavate the area. Continue to excavate about one foot wider than the outline.

4. In order to level the area, remove rocks and roots and fill depressions. Level and tamp the area. Further compact the area by wetting it.

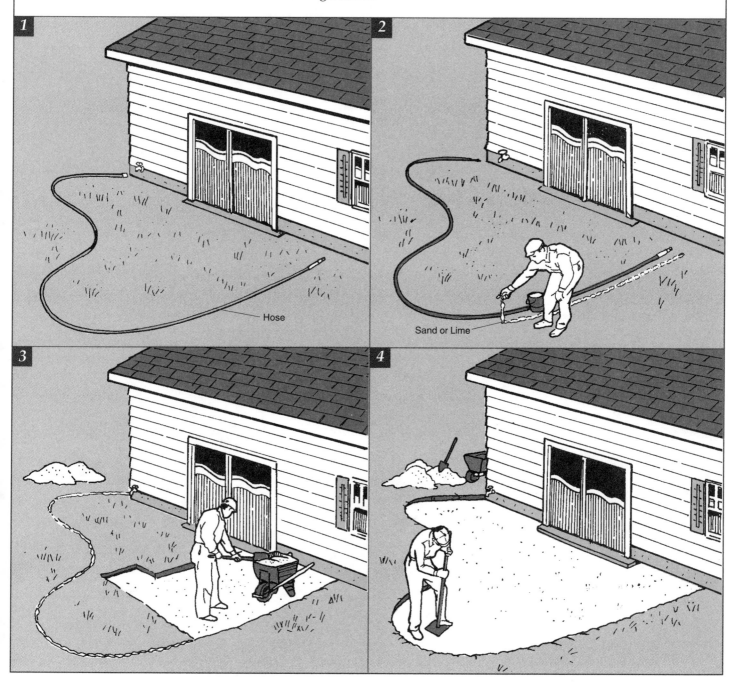

Hose

Sand or Lime

Building the Forms

1 Digging Trenches. From the corners where the patio meets the house, dig trenches out to the furthest points of patio. The trenches should be just outside the excavation area. They should be as deep as the edging form and 2 inches wider.

In one trench place a 2x12 board, cut to the proper length according to the patio design. Begin staking the area at the corner end closest to the foundation. Drive stakes (scrap boards make good stakes) approximately 24 to 30 inches apart.

2 Marking Level. Using a carpenter's level, level the edge board until it is level with the mark on the house foundation (this also will be the height marked on the interior stake).

At the furthest corner, move the beam down, following the pitch that has been graded for drainage. The top of the form board should align with the string lines.

3 Attaching the Stakes. Now attach the first stake to the board with double-headed nails. Make sure that the stakes are on the outside of the board. They should be flush with or below the forms. Repeat this operation for the board on the other side of the patio.

4 Bracing the Forms. Take the remaining board and connect it to the outside corners of the two side pieces. Butting the two boards tightly, nail the stake to both form boards. Each corner should be braced. Stake the 2x4s around the entire perimeter you have laid out. The stake height should be just below the top of the board.

The stakes at the two farthest corners will be the same height relative to the foundation as those nearer the house, but will actually be longer due to the grade. Cut all stakes off just below form height. You have now set the exterior formwork.

With the dirt that was removed during initial excavation, fill in around the outside of the boards. Make sure the dirt is tamped against the forms; this will prevent unwanted movement of the form boards. On the inside of the form, tamp the earth so it is level with the bottom of the form board; if necessary, relevel and regrade the entire area within the form, compacting or filling.

5 Securing Permanent Forms. If your design calls for a grid-like design, stake the permanent (inner) forms. Then, drive nails into the forms. This will help hold the concrete.

1 Drive stakes approximately 24 to 30 in. apart.

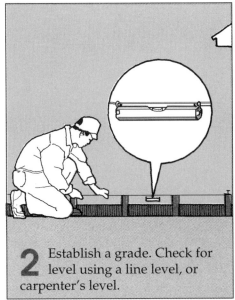

2 Establish a grade. Check for level using a line level, or carpenter's level.

3 Attach the stakes to the form boards using double-headed nails.

4 Brace the form at each corner and any weak spots that you may find.

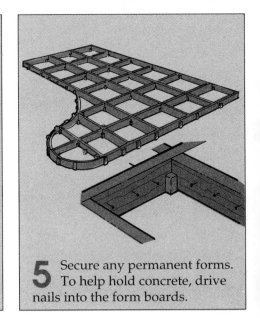

5 Secure any permanent forms. To help hold concrete, drive nails into the form boards.

Creating Curved Forms

Your patio design may call for curved forms. If so, you can use 1-inch lumber rather than 2 inch. You also may use 1/4- to 1/2-inch-thick plywood, sheet metal, or hardboard. Gentler, short-radius curves can use 2-inch-thick wood forms that have been saw-kerfed and then bent until the kerfs are held closed; or you can bend plywood, with the grain vertical. Wet lumber will be easier to bend than will dry lumber. For very tight curves, use 3/8-inch redwood or plywood bender boards. Sandwich together two or three boards against the stakes, and nail into position. Vertical curves also can be formed by saw kerfing. Another option is to bend the 2x4s during staking. When the slope changes sharply, shorter lengths of forming are best.

Lay out the curve with a string line that is tied to temporary stakes. Then adjust the line up or down on the stakes to give a smooth curve. Short lengths of the forming are then set to the string line and are staked securely. To keep forms at proper curvature and grade, set the stakes closer on curves than on straight runs.

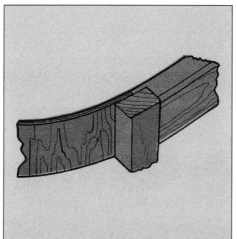

Use a 2x4 stake when connecting a straight and a curved form.

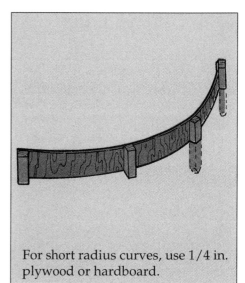

For short radius curves, use 1/4 in. plywood or hardboard.

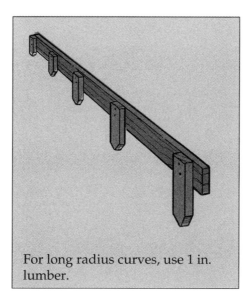

For long radius curves, use 1 in. lumber.

Two-by lumber can be saw-kerfed and bent so that the cuts close.

Creating Permanent Forms

Permanent forms are those that are installed along and across the slab of concrete. They may be wood strips, brick or even concrete block. Not only do these strips add texture and pattern, they also act as control joints. The wood used for permanent forms should be treated with preservative. Redwood, cypress or cedar are good types of wood to use.

Assemble the permanent forms with care. Miter corner joints and neatly butt intersecting strips. Do not drive nails through the tops of permanent forms. To anchor the outside forms to the concrete, drive 16d galvanized nails in a horizontal row, from the outside, midway up the form boards. Space the nails 16 inches apart. Interior divider strips require similarly spaced nail anchors, but drive them in from alternate sides of the board. All nail heads should be flush with the forms. Stake the forms as needed to hold their shape and position; then drive the stakes at least 2 inches below the tops of the forms (or cut them off) so they will not show once the slab is complete. Mask the tops of the boards with tape to protect them from stains and abrasions from the concrete.

Set the stakes closer on curves than on straight runs (about 18 to 24 in. apart).

Preparing to Pour

1 Using Isolation Joints.
Isolation joints are used to separate a new concrete pour from other already existing materials, such as wood, brick or old concrete. The joint is a preformed material that is about 1/2 inch wide. This material allows for differing rates of expansion and contraction.

2 Oiling the Forms. If you are going to reuse the forms, use an inexpensive grade of motor oil or an oil spray to coat the interior part of the form. This helps later in the removal of the form. If the forms are to be permanent, protect the edges with masking tape.

3 Preparing the Base. Place approximately 6 inches of gravel over the entire area contained within the forms. Your reference point will be the top of the form board. Lay it down in two layers of 3 inches each. Make sure that each layer is tamped thoroughly until firm.The 6-inch depth of the gravel should be tamped down to 4 inches.

4 Screeding the Base. Place the sand uniformly over the entire gravel area in a 2-inch layer. Screed the sand until it is completely level. Use concrete build-up as fill for any low places and tamp it lightly.Tamp the sand down. If the gravel shows through, do not be alarmed. Place enough sand so that a difference between the top of the sand and the top of the form board will be approximately 4 inches.

At this point the edge beam must be created. Remove the earth from the inside perimeter of the form board for a width of 6 inches and depth of 6 inches; leaving about 2 inches of gravel and sand on the bottom. It will be excavated to just below the bottom edge of the form board. Moisten the area so the shape holds.

1 Use an isolation joint to separate the new concrete from other existing material, such as the house foundation.

2 Forms that will be reused should be covered with a layer of oil. Protect edges of permanent forms with masking tape.

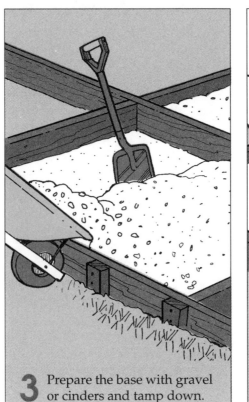

3 Prepare the base with gravel or cinders and tamp down.

4 Screed the sand base until it is completely level.

Adding Reinforcing Mesh

1. When set on soil that may heave or shift, the patio or walk will require reinforcing mesh. This also is the case with a subgrade of very wet or sandy soil. The mesh will not prevent cracking but it will hold the cracks tightly closed. The mesh is size 6/6 and 10/10, which means it is made of welded 1.0-gauge wire having 6-inch square openings. It comes in rolls. Have a helper stand on one end of the roll while you unroll it.

2. Cut the mesh to fit using large fencing pliers, heavy bolt cutters or electrical side cutters.

3. Take pains to flatten the mesh thoroughly so it will not be near the top or bottom surface on the pour. This can be done simply by walking on it.

4. Before placing the mesh, set small stones on the base to raise it up about 2 inches below the top of the form— or the approximate center of the

concrete pour. Position the mesh on top of the rocks. At this point you should avoid walking on the mesh.

5. Do not allow the mesh to come into contact with the form, or you will have a piece of metal sticking out the side of the concrete. This will later rust and discolor.

6. Wet the area the day before the concrete is to be poured. Then, spritz it again just before the concrete is poured.

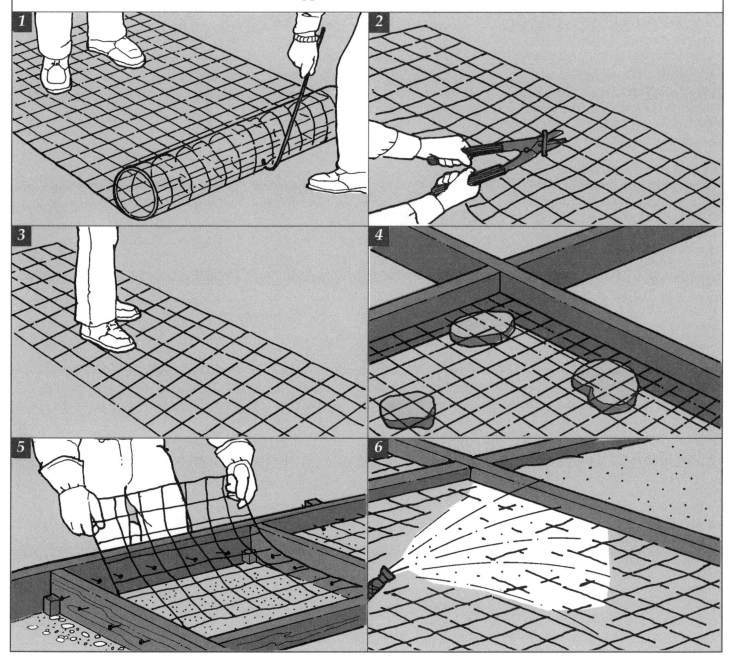

Pouring the Concrete

Regardless of whether you hand mix, use a portable mixer, or purchase the concrete from a transit mix company, the method of casting is the same.

1 Beginning to Pour. Start as far back in the form as you can, and spread the back area first. You will need to build a bridge in order for the wheelbarrow to transport the mixture to the areas.

2 Spreading the Concrete. A hoe or rake is easier to use than a shovel because you can easily pull the material in place and lift the rake out. You will have to use a shovel in some instances to lift material and move it back in odd areas.

Since you will probably have to get right in there in the mix in order to move it around, you will need rubber hip boots, preferably without buckles.

3 Pouring the Concrete. Do not dump loads of concrete on top of each other or separate from each other. Succeeding loads should be dumped against each other. Using the rake tines, pull up the reinforcing mesh. Fill all forms to their top edges. Pay attention to corners, edges of forms, or any turns or curves in forms. Spade the concrete to remove air pockets.

4 Screeding the Surface. Select a straight 2x4. If it is slightly warped, the warp must bow up rather than down. A downward bow will create a surface that will hold puddles. A slight upward bow will provide drainage.

Starting at the back end of the pour, move the screed towards the front to strike off excess concrete. Move the screed back and forth sideways to help it "slide" through the concrete. The correct process not only removes excess concrete, but also pushes larger pieces of aggregate down below the surface. Use the shovel to fill low spots with an excess cement. Then screed again.

1 Start pouring the concrete as far back in the form as you possibly can.

2 Use a hoe or rake to spread the concrete. Use a shovel to move concrete into odd areas.

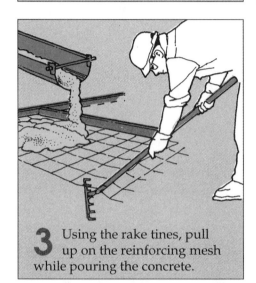

3 Using the rake tines, pull up on the reinforcing mesh while pouring the concrete.

4 Using a straight 2x4, carefully screed the concrete surface.

Construction Joints

There are cases when you will not pour the entire slab of concrete at once. First, the forms are erected, then a section is closed off with a temporary form board called a stopboard. The section is filled with concrete, screeded and finished. Once the concrete has set, but not before it has cured; the stopboard is removed, the joint edge is oiled and another portion is filled.

The joint between the initial and the later section is called a construction joint. This joint also can function as a control joint, so plan the position of all construction joints to correspond to control joint dimensions dictated by your project.

Adding butted joints. If the slab is to be 4 inches thick or less, you only need a butted joint. The stopboard is made the same way as an interior form board. Some projects require tie rods to bind the slabs together.

Adding keyed joints. If the slab is 5 inches thick or more, create a keyed joint. The stopboard made with a shaping device attached all the way across its center. The edge of the pour will take on the shape of this key, creating a groove across the edge of the slab. When the second section is poured, the pour fills the shape of the key. This joint prevents the two slabs from shifting separately and maintains a level surface.

5 Floating the Concrete. The first step in finishing the concrete is floating the surface of the concrete. This step levels the concrete, pushing aggregates beneath the surface. Floating can be done with a bullfloat or darby, and may be followed by a hand float if necessary. The bullfloat is used on large surfaces, such as patios. It removes excess water from the surface and knocks down the small ridges left by the screeding operation, leaving the pour smooth and level. Push and pull the large bullfloat back and forth over the concrete. At the end of each stroke, lift the float and move it over to make another parallel stroke. When pushing it forward, tilt it a little so the front edge is raised; when pulling backward, tilt the back edge up just a little to prevent the edge of the bullfloat from digging into the concrete. This is the hardest part of the job.

6 Using a Darby. On smaller jobs (such as walkways) in which you can reach across or at least to the center of the job from each side, use a darby. This is a smaller, two-handed float that is used in a circular motion. Again, make sure you do not allow the edges or corners to dig into the wet concrete and do not over-float. When water starts to bleed onto the surface of the slab, it is done.

7 Using an Edger. Surfaces of walks and patios should have round, smooth edges. This keeps the slab from chipping as badly as it would if it had sharp edges. It also is safer to walk on and it looks better. First, separate the form and the concrete by sandwiching a trowel blade between them. Then, run a hand-edger back and forth along the edges of the pour, holding the tool flat on the surface and against the wood form. Be careful not to dig the edger into the wet concrete.

8 Placing Control Joints. Cutting control joints is actually done in much the same way as edging; however, the reasons for having them are different. Not only do the grooves break up the appearance of a huge slab of concrete, but they also provide a place for the concrete to crack should it settle and shift. This sounds terrible, but a crack in one of the joints will follow the groove rather than occurring randomly. The result is a good-looking, durable surface. Without the control joint, the concrete will still crack, but the crack is liable to have a jagged, uneven appearance.

Lay a 2-inch-thick board across the slab. Then, using the board as a guide, take a jointing tool and run it across the slab. The spacing of control joints will differ according to the various projects, as will be discussed in detail for each type. The depth of the joint, which is dictated by the kind and size of the project, also is very important. The rule is that the groove should be one-fourth the thickness of the concrete slab.

5 Create a smooth, level surface by floating the concrete. This is done with a tool called a bullfloat.

6 Use a darby to float smaller areas that you can reach across.

7 Run a hand-edger back and forth along the edges of the pour, being careful not to dig the edger into the wet concrete.

8 To prevent jagged, unsightly cracks, create control joints in the concrete. Control joints are strategically placed grooves.

Slick Troweling. Test the surface before finishing the slab. Scrape the slab with a steel trowel; if wetness appears, then it is not ready.

For a really slick, hard finish, smooth the concrete with a steel trowel. Apply it with the same circular motion as used when floating, keeping the edge lifted slightly with each pass so you do not cut into the surface of the concrete. Sprinkling the surface with a bit of water will help provide an even slicker finish, but do not overdo it. Use slight pressure on the trowel to get the best finish; trowelling three times or until the surface feels silky smooth without any gritty feel of sand.

Once the troweling has been completed, go back over the edges and grooves to lightly clean off any excess moisture and cement that might have been forced down into them. A hand brush can be used for this. Be careful to keep the edges of the tools from cutting into the freshly troweled cement.

Rough Troweling. To produce a rough, skidproof finish, trowel the slab with a wooden trowel or float. This tool works the same way a steel trowel works, except you only need to make one or two passes. Move the trowel freely, forming a series of arcs.

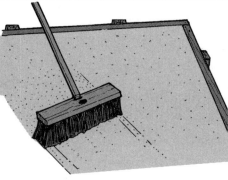

Broomed Finish. Brooming should be done after edging and floating. A stiff-bristle shop broom works best. The most difficult part is to avoid digging the bristles into the surface and marring it. Pull the broom across the surface. Lift it after each stroke and move to the opposite side. Broom the surface at right angles to the traffic pattern.

Exposed Aggregate. Use rounded gravel of a uniform size and shape. Press them into the concrete with a float board until they are not visible. After concrete has begun to set, hose and scrub surface with a broom, until the tops of gravel show. Let concrete set for four days. Wearing protective clothing, wash surface with a solution of 1:5 muriatic acid and water. Then, rinse the area.

Curing Concrete

The concrete must be kept at a favorable temperature and moisture level for a certain length of time. Allow the slab to set for 4 or 5 hours; then dampen it with a fine mist from a garden hose. If the water pressure is too high, you will wash out the finish. Cover the concrete with pieces of burlap, old newspapers or polyethylene sheets soaked with water. Keep them well soaked for at least 3 days at the proper temperature. If the temperature goes below 50 degrees, continue curing for another 3 days. Most contractors like to continue curing for a week.

After about 10 days, the forms may be stripped from the job and any backfilling with earth completed.

WORKING WITH BRICK MASONRY

Brick is a very popular material for the do-it-yourselfer. It is laid in place one unit at a time by hand, and does not require as much physical effort as concrete block or stone. Bricklaying can be an enjoyable job. It is easily learned, and even a first-timer can produce a pleasing finished project. Since the work is done a little at a time, even a big job does not seem so awesome a task.

Brick Characteristics

A brick is a small individual building unit made of clay. Those made today have changed little in design and manufacture from those that were produced thousands of years ago. The main difference is that the old bricks were sun baked or dried in the sun, but today's bricks are heated in a kiln to harden them and to make them more resistant to moisture and weathering. The standard size of 2¼x3¾x8 inches has not changed significantly from the days when brick makers figured out that the unit was just about the right size to handle easily with one hand. Today's bricks are made of a much wider variety of clay types than the older bricks, so there are more variations in the bricks produced.

Some bricks are the natural color of the different clays after firing. They can range from gray, light tan, light or dark red, or even purple. In other cases, ceramic glazes are applied to bricks. The popularity of used brick, taken from demolished old buildings, has resulted in the manufacture of new "used" bricks that are made by adding a bit of lime and sand or cement to clay, then tumbling the finished bricks in a giant tumbler to crumble and break away their sharp edges and to give them an aged appearance.

The finish of bricks can vary from rough sand to ultra-smooth. In addition, stamping machines and embossed rollers will apply designs to the facing sides of the bricks as the bricks are cut to shape. These designs can give the effect of logs, stones, or even sculpture.

Types of Bricks

Although there are a great number of different kinds of bricks, there are four basic types used in most modern construction. Check local building codes to find what type of bricks may be used in your part of the country for particular projects.

Building or Common Brick. This is the most economical and popular brick. It can be used for almost any type of construction. Because the color and dimensional size of common brick varies, this would not be the choice for projects such as a fireplace front, requiring a very uniform brick. There also are more imperfections in this type of brick and some of them may be chipped, broken or warped. Still, they serve well for patios, garden walls, barbecues, or projects that require a "used" brick finish. Building or common bricks are available in three different grades.

■ *SW.* This brick will withstand severe weathering such as freezing, thawing or rain-and-freeze conditions. These are the most expensive grade of common brick.

■ *MW.* This grade withstands modest weathering, including some rain and freezing, but cannot be used in areas of severe weathering.

■ *NW.* These bricks can be used in mild climates where there is no danger from freezing or frost. They also are suitable for frost areas, but only if the bricks are protected from rain or moisture. The least expensive kind of common brick, they are quite commonly used for interior jobs.

Choose the most economical brick for your particular area.

Face Brick. Face brick is the best quality brick. It is manufactured so that all bricks are quite uniform in color, size, texture, and face surface. The faces themselves range in style from a glazed china-like surface in a number of color choices to an imprinted pattern resembling stone or other types of materials. There are few defects in this type of brick. It is usually not any stronger than common brick, but because of the extra amount of manufacturing care, the units will usually better withstand the effects of weather than will common brick.

Paving Brick. Paving brick is extremely strong and sturdy. It is made to be used without mortar for such things as courtyards or driveways. The paving brick is composed of special types of clays that are baked at higher temperatures and for a longer time than other brick types. The result is a very durable and strong brick.

Firebrick. Firebrick is made of a special clay and is heated to an extremely high temperature to make the units resistant to high heat. Firebrick is used primarily to line fireplaces, ovens and furnaces. It is a pale yellow and is installed with special fireclay mortars.

Brick Sizes

One confusing aspect of ordering bricks is the nomenclature concerning their size. They may be referred to in nominal size or by their actual size. The nominal size, however, also includes figures for an average mortar joint. Since mortar joints can vary a great deal, the nominal figure can be misleading. Ask for the bricks by their actual size. Then include measurements for the mortar joint in your particular project to help you figure the needs of your project.

In an ordinary run of bricks, there may be as much as 1/2-inch difference between brick sizes; therefore, merely measuring a brick off a pile in the brickyard will not enable you to figure the job properly. Ask your dealer for the actual sizes of the specific brick you plan to use.

Design Considerations

Once you have decided to use brick as the surface material, you will need to select the pattern, color and texture, as well as the size of the brick. The range of brick paving sizes is enormous. You also must decide if you wish to have a patio with or without joints. The joints between the bricks can be used very effectively for pattern purposes; a brick patio where the joints are not accented can create a uniform appearance. The number of bricks you need will depend upon the size of brick and the patio pattern chosen.

Probably one of the easiest, most enjoyable and practical methods for constructing a walk or patio is with bricks. In fact, once you have the materials on hand, the work is so simple that you can complete a typical job during a weekend.

The patio or walk can be constructed of bricks laid in a mortar bed on a concrete footing or in a sand bed over a gravel base. Often, brick installations such as these feature permanent edging materials, such as bricks set on end, special wood beams, or even old railroad ties (see pages 65-68). The edging holds the shape of the patio and increases its longevity.

Be versatile when you plan your project. If the patio meets a backyard fence, leave an open area between the two. Later, fill in the area with a raised planting bed to blend the fence and the patio.

Rather than removing trees or shrubs, build the patio around them. Each tree or plant will need an open area equal to at least 1½ to 2 feet in diameter. This allows an adequate amount of moisture to reach the roots and enough space to grow. For a raised patio, surround a tree with a well made of dry-laid concrete block. Then add gravel to the desired height.

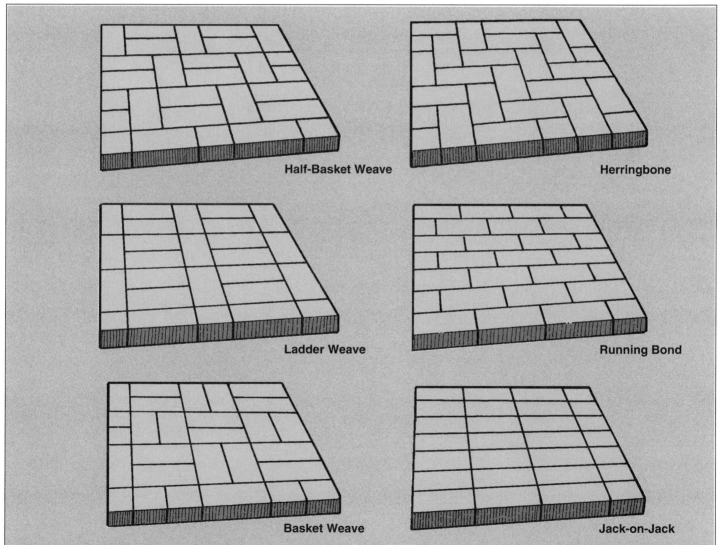

Half-Basket Weave　　**Herringbone**

Ladder Weave　　**Running Bond**

Basket Weave　　**Jack-on-Jack**

Choosing a Brick Pattern. Once you have made the decision to use bricks as the material for your patio or walk, you must make a decision on the color, texture and size of the brick you would like to use. The bricks can be laid in one of many different patterns.

Laying Brick in Sand

Laying brick in a bed of sand is by far the easiest way to create a patio or walk. If you follow the proper procedures, and if the climate is mild, the job will last as long as if laid in a bed of mortar. Pay careful attention to proper grading and installation of the sand bed, or else the project will look shoddy and haphazard. Remember, too, that no matter how carefully you work on the sand bed, it will still settle somewhat, resulting in depressions in the brick surface after the job has been completed. To remedy the problem, remove the bricks that have sunk down, place more sand beneath them and replace them.

1 Excavating and Formwork.

One of the main prerequisites to creating a good-looking, long-lasting paved walk or patio is a solid, well-packed subsurface. In many instances, you need only cut away the turf to the depth necessary to accommodate 2 inches of sand and the thickness (or part of it) of the bricks. The paving material often reaches as much as 2 inches above ground level.

Since the brick design will rest directly on the sand and gravel subbase, a permanently treated wood edger will be required. For purposes of demonstration, a 2x10 board that has been treated for below grade will be used. Measuring against the house foundation, measure the 12x16-foot patio area and mark the desired height of the brick surface. Place the treated 2x12s into the excavated area but on the outside of the 12- and 16-foot dimensions. In addition, place another board against the house foundation. The inside dimensions of the forms should be 12x16 feet. Nail the corners together and recheck all dimensions. The bracing stakes can be eliminated, since the brick and the earth infill will be enough to stabilize the edging boards. The boards will follow the graded pitch so that water will run off away from the house. Having set the boards around the perimeter of the patio area, infill and tamp the soil against the formwork. You may want to string a line from the corner stakes to act as a patio height guide.

If you use a temporary edger, it need not be treated wood—or, excavate deeper and set the top of the brick flush with ground level, using no form other than undisturbed earth.

Expansion Joints. In severe winter areas, expansion joints will reduce frost heave. Put joints every 8 to 10 feet, preferably as squares, and where dissimilar materials meet. Prepare a pattern on paper first.

2 Installing the Edging.

Permanent wood borders must be made of cypress, redwood or other wood that has been pressure-treated. After the excavation is complete, install the edging so that the top edge is just above, or flush with, the ground level. To anchor the edging solidly in place, install stakes made of the same material as the forms. Nail the forms to the stakes with duplex-headed nails. Fill in the base and the sand bed; lay the bricks. Finish as desired. Remove the nails from the stakes. Using a wedge-shaped piece of 2x4, pound the permanent stakes below ground level. Do not hammer the edging itself. Cover the stakes with soil.

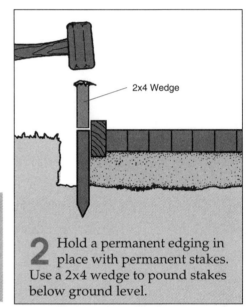
2x4 Wedge

2 Hold a permanent edging in place with permanent stakes. Use a 2x4 wedge to pound stakes below ground level.

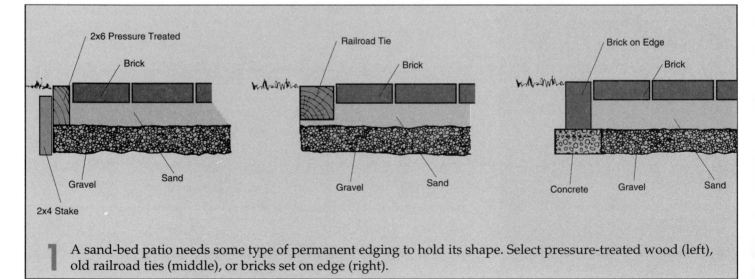

1 A sand-bed patio needs some type of permanent edging to hold its shape. Select pressure-treated wood (left), old railroad ties (middle), or bricks set on edge (right).

3 **Adding the Base.** Since the brick, if placed flat on its side, is only 2¼ inches thick for a standard modular brick, you will need to place the gravel in the form until it is 4 inches from the top of the form. If you will be placing the brick on edge, 6 inches must be allowed from the top of the form to the top of the compacted gravel.

You can use a rake to level out any uneven portions of surface. After placing the gravel and tamping or compacting it in the form, the surface is then ready for the next course.

After the edging has been secured, place and tamp gravel fill. Then add a layer of sand that is at least 2 inches deep. Spread the sand roughly in place with a rake. With a hose set on fine spray, thoroughly dampen the sand. In a short time, the sand will settle. Fill in the spots that are obviously low and dampen down the new fill.

While the sand is still wet, pull a screed across the edging to level the sand bed. Remove any excess sand and fill in low spots as you go. Hose down the sand bed again after leveling. Use a fine mist so you do not dislodge the sand.

4 **Pitching the Patio.** If the patio or walk is located adjacent to the foundation of your home, and you are in a climate where rain and snow are prevalent, the surface should be gently pitched away from the foundation at a rate of no less than 1/8 inch per foot of slab width. This is a minimal amount and is acceptable in climates where the annual rainfall is slight. In a wetter climate, it is desirable to use 1/4 inch per foot of slab. For example, if the patio will have a width of 12 feet extending from the foundation of your home, at 1/4 inch per foot the total drop across the width would be 3 inches.

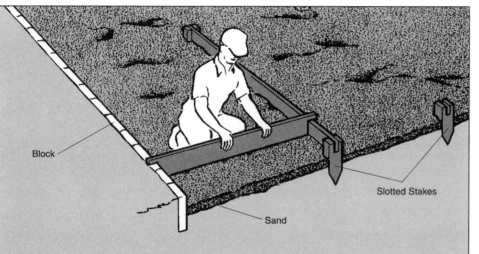

3 Ensure a level sand bed for pavers. Set up wooden forms or patio blocks as edgings, add sand, and put up temporary wood strips fastened to 2x2 stakes every 4 ft. Notch a 1x6 at ends to same thickness as edging; use to level sand, resting one end on edging, the other on wood strip.

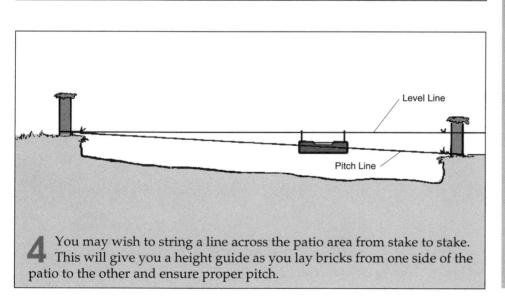

4 You may wish to string a line across the patio area from stake to stake. This will give you a height guide as you lay bricks from one side of the patio to the other and ensure proper pitch.

Crowning a Walk

The paved surface must be constructed so water can run off. Although some moisture will soak down through the cracks between the bricks, you still need a way for most of the surface water to drain away quickly. To provide the necessary pitch to a walk, the center is crowned (somewhat raised in the center). Crowning also adds another benefit to a brick walk. Since the traffic along a walk eventually will drive and pack down the center, crowning prevents the center of the walk from becoming lower than the edges.

Crown the sand by creating a drag-board that is higher in the center than at the ends. Cut the dragboard to produce the appropriate amount of pitch.

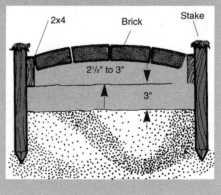

5 **Splitting the Bricks.** Edgings, or the size and shape of your patio, may require that you split some of the bricks. To split bricks, use a bricker's chisel and a heavy hammer. (A 3-pound sledge with a 10-inch handle works well). Set the chisel across the middle of the brick and strike hard. The brick will split neatly. You may substitute brick edge blocks or railroad ties for the treated wood edger to keep the bricks in place.

6 **Placing the Brick.** Beginning in one corner, place the bricks in the pattern you desire. Tie a mason's line to guide you in laying the bricks neatly and in a straight line. Leave a 3/8-inch joint between each brick. Carefully place bricks into position, or you will displace the sand, and create a base that is not level. Use a level and a straightedge to check for level as you go. If a brick is too low, pick it up and add more sand to the base. Try not to go back to an area already worked on, as you may disturb the spacing.

To create a traditional running bond pattern, place the first row of bricks end-to-end. Start the second row with a half-brick, followed by whole bricks placed end-to-end and a final half-brick. Start the third row with a whole brick. This creates a pattern where the end joints fall mid-way between bricks of the previous row. Repeat the pattern for following rows.

If you have chosen a two- or three-brick basket-weave pattern, see page 49 for instructions.

7 **Setting the Brick.** Start at one corner of the project. Position the brick in the desired pattern. To embed the bricks into the sand, lay a 16-inch piece of 2x6 over the bricks and hammer them down with a large mallet. Run a long level or straightedge across the surface to be sure that the finished surface is level to the edging and that the bricks are level with each other. Set the paving bricks 1/4 to 1/2 inch higher than the desired final height of the finished surface, since the bricks will settle after a time. Butt the bricks, or allow for consistently sized joints between the pavers. You may have to tap them together in some areas. When tapping, protect the surface of the brick with a buffer board; the hammer can chip, crack or break the units.

8 **Filling the Joints.** After laying the bricks, start in one corner and spread dry sand on the surface. Sweep the sand down into the cracks between the pavers. Work on one quarter at a time, sweeping from all directions to fill all the joints completely. Then, lightly hose the surface to pack down the dry sand and clean off any excess. Repeat this process until the joints are completely filled. From time to time, you will have to sweep in more sand to keep soil and weeds from working up through the joints.

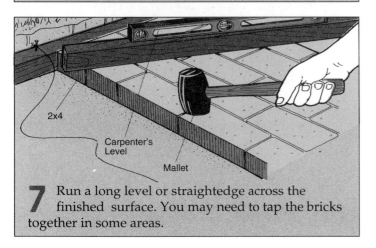

5 To cut a brick, locate the place for the cut, scribe a line around the brick at that point, place a brick chisel on the line, and strike the chisel with a mallet.

6 Always work from a corner outward. The brick should be placed on edge in an alternating basket weave pattern.

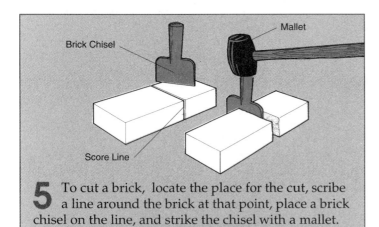

7 Run a long level or straightedge across the finished surface. You may need to tap the bricks together in some areas.

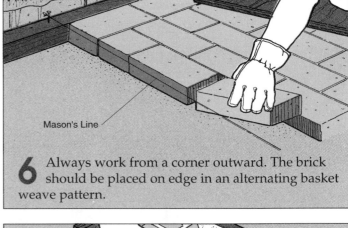

8 Spread dry sand across the surface of the bricks. Sweep the sand down into the cracks between the pavers, filling the joints completely.

Dry Mortar Joint Fill

You can place mortar in the joints of a sand-bed patio if you wish, but the mortar joints will crack and will not look as neat as the sand-filled joints. Mortar the joints by applying a dry mix of 1 part cement and 4 parts sand. Brush the dry mix in and around the bricks. Pack all joints with the dry mortar; moisten the mortar by spraying it with a garden hose. Continue the light spray for half an hour. Do not flush away any of the mortar with high water pressure. Over the next few days, dampen the surface once again. The cement will bond with the sand to form a hard joint. Repeat the process every year.

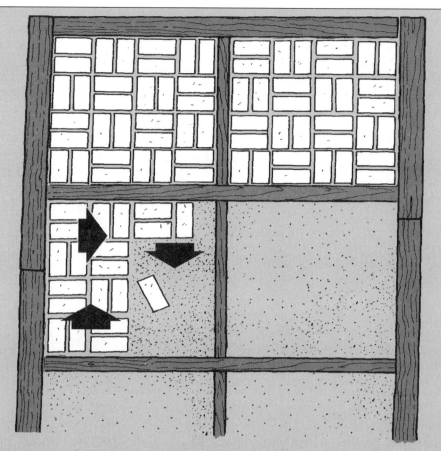

Laying Brick Patterns. Begin installing bricks at lower left corner and work clockwise within each wood form. Use the bricks as a surface from which to work as you lay the units.

Laying Brick Patterns

There are several patterns used in brick patios and walks. The careful layout required for any horizontal brick surface is obvious. There are several variations of the basket weave pattern.

Laying the Basket Weave Design.

A basket weave pattern is based upon blocks of brick set on edge at right angles to each other. Each block must be of equal size. Arrange joint sizes so that the two or three bricks set in one direction equal the length of the brick.

Three-Brick Basket Weave.

Beginning in one corner, place three bricks on edge. All should run in the same direction and there should be a 3/8-inch joint left between them. The size of the block will equal the length of the bricks ($7^5/_8$ inches), which

should equal the sum of the three thicknesses and the two mortar joints ($2^1/_4$+3/8+$2^1/_4$+3/8+$2^1/_4$) to yield a $7^5/_8$x$7^5/_8$-inch square.

Now set the second block of three bricks at right angles to the first block. To assure the correct spacing, align the top and bottom brick with the top and bottom edges of the lengthwise brick they butt against. To complete the block, center the third brick between the two. Continue alternating blocks, working out and across the patio area. Try not to go back to an area already completed, since you may disturb the spacing.

Two-Brick Basket Weave.

If you prefer to lay the bricks flat rather than on edge, each block will contain only two bricks. Again, work on aligning outside edges to create equal squares.

Laying Brick in Mortar

Brick may be set in a bed of mortar over a clean, solid and well drained concrete surface (see pages 29-40). In fact, this is one way to refurbish an old concrete patio.

1 Preparing the Brick. Brick absorbs moisture quite readily, and unless it is wetted down before it is laid, it will virtually suck the moisture out of the mortar. If a joint dries too rapidly, the mortar is weakened and does not properly adhere the bricks. The bricks do not need to be soaked. If they are dripping wet when they are laid the mortar mix may become too wet.

There is a simple test you can use to determine whether the bricks are wet enough. In a 1-inch diameter circle on the brick face, place several drops of water. If the moisture disappears in less than one minute, spray all the bricks with a garden hose before you mix the mortar. Continue until water runs out from the pile. By the time you get the mortar mixed, the surface moisture should have evaporated from the bricks and they should be ready to use.

2 Testing with a Dry Run. Lay out the project without mortar so you can determine the best arrangement. Use a nail to cut scratches into the concrete footing to indicate brick positions. Snap a chalk line or use a crayon to mark final locations for the bricks.

Lay as many full bricks as possible, end-to-end or in the pattern chosen. Use thin wooden strips as spacers to allow for the size of the mortar joints. Note the size of the closure brick. If possible, modify your plan so that the closure brick will be a full unit and there will not be any cutting necessary.

3 Preparing the Mortar Base. Prepare a standard mortar mix, lay and screed a 1/2-inch mortar bed. The procedure is similar to screeding sand (see page 38). Screed only 3 square feet at a time. Never mix more mortar than you can use in one hour.

4 Placing the Brick. Lay the bricks in the mortar in one of the patterns shown on page 45. Butter the ends and one side, position and tap each brick firmly to avoid air pockets. Leave a 1/2-inch-wide mortar joint between each brick and between the courses.

5 Setting the Bricks. Use a level and a long straightedge to ensure that all bricks are level—high or low spots will cause water pooling. Make sure there are no air pockets trapped in the mortar below the bricks; frost will cause bricks to heave in the area around an empty air pocket.

6 Filling the Joints. You can trowel the joints flush with the bricks or tool the joints slightly.

Tooled joints, however, should not be made too deep, or the surface will be hard to keep clean.

Position the mortar near at hand so you do not have to reach very far for it. If you can't get the wheelbarrow close enough to the job, use a mortar hawk and holder to hold a smaller amount close at hand.

■ turn the trowel sideways 90 degrees so the blade is straight up and down;

■ at the same time, give a slightly downward flip of the trowel.

When the mortar is thrown or flung in this manner, the mortar adheres well to the surface and settles down in any depressions.

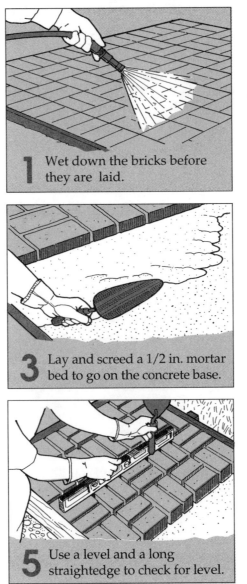

1 Wet down the bricks before they are laid.

3 Lay and screed a 1/2 in. mortar bed to go on the concrete base.

5 Use a level and a long straightedge to check for level.

2 Use a thin, wooden strip as a spacer between bricks.

4 Lay the bricks in the pattern you have chosen.

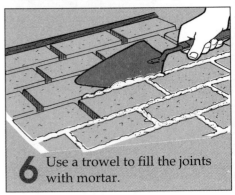

6 Use a trowel to fill the joints with mortar.

WORKING WITH STONE MASONRY

There is a sense of immortality that goes along with creating structures with stone. Many people say that no other type of manual labor gives as much satisfaction. And rightly so; as there are many centuries old stone structures that are not only standing today, but just as sturdy and beautiful as they were 100 years or more ago. Almost any type of stonework you do around your home will add to its value and beauty.

Types of Stone

Stone can be used for many different projects including a patio or garden walk. It blends with almost any decor, from traditional to formal to rustic landscaping.

Stonework is not easy. In fact, it is backbreaking work, and you should not try to do too much in one day. The do-it-yourselfer who follows this age-old rule can accomplish quite a bit. Fortunately, one of the real advantages of working with stone, is that you can quit work at almost any time. In fact, some jobs require these time intervals to prevent too much weight from being applied before the mortar sets up. Stonework is a good project for the do-it-yourselfer who may only have a couple of hours to spare each day.

There are many different kinds of stone. The type you use depends on your project, and the types of stone available in your area. Because of their great weight, it is impractical to ship stones a great distance. The stones most often chosen for use in construction projects are granite, limestone, marble, slate, flagstone, sandstone, gneiss and tap rock. The stones come either as quarried stone or fieldstone.

Flagstone

Flagstone is a classic material that is both beautiful and functional and quite expensive as well. The stone is made up of the following mild earth colors: yellow, brownish yellow, orange, red, gray. However, designing in color is always more difficult than in monotones; therefore, cast concrete flagstone is often used instead of the real thing. The imitation stone enables greater control of color, surface texture and shape, but for some, only the genuine stone will do.

Quarried Stone

Quarried stone, cut and shaped, is used for more formal projects. It is cut and slabbed at the quarry, but the face of the stone is left natural. Formal patios usually are made of slate or flagstone; both are quarried materials.

Fieldstone

A rock retaining wall for an informal garden often would be constructed of fieldstone, or stones picked up from a field or dry creek bottom. Depending on shape and quality, they can also be used for informal walks and patios.

Masonry Tools

Stonework is one of the few crafts that requires little more than a strong back. In some instances, you may have to put down a concrete footing to hold the stonework, in which case you will need concrete-working tools. However, for working with dry-laid stone you will need nothing more than a tape measure, a shovel with a sharp blade, a brick or stone mason's hammer, a chisel and a wheelbarrow. A large pry bar helps move larger rocks. Wear a pair of heavy-duty leather gloves, and use safety glasses when you split stones.

Naturally, for mortared stonework you need tools for making and applying mortar, just as for concrete block or brickwork. You also will need a carpenter's level, a string line and a string level.

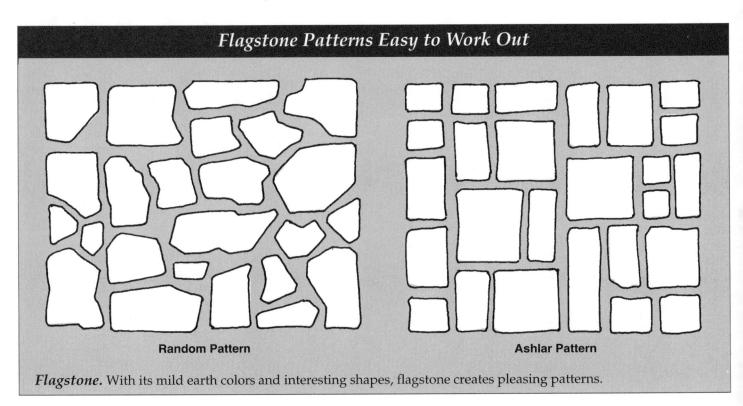

Flagstone Patterns Easy to Work Out

Random Pattern

Ashlar Pattern

Flagstone. With its mild earth colors and interesting shapes, flagstone creates pleasing patterns.

Finding or Buying the Stones

Most likely, you will have to purchase the stone for your project. Before designing the project, visit the quarry and natural stone yards to determine what they have on hand. With this knowledge you can design the project to suit the particular types of stone available.

Relative Costs

The most expensive stone is cut stone. If you are looking for a carefully fitted, formal design, this is the stone you will need. Purchasing stones that are a uniform size and color is an expense. In most instances the quarry will have the stones graded according to color and uniformity of shape. Rubble stone, the debris left from blasting and cutting the cut stone, is more economical.

Buying the Right Amount

To determine the amount of stone you will need, figure the cubic volume of the project in feet by multiplying length x width x height. Stone is sold by the cubic yard. After determining the cubic feet you have in the project, divide the number of cubic feet in the wall by 27 to determine the cubic yards of stone needed. If you are buying selected cut stone, take the cubic volume and add about 10 percent to account for breakage and waste. When buying rubble stone (which usually is dumped in the back of a truck for delivery) you will need to add at least 25 percent extra for breakage and waste.

Another factor is whether you plan to construct the project using a dry-laid stone, or a mortar-and-stone technique. Dry-laid stone projects will require better joint fits, since there is no mortar to help bind the stones together. We will discuss each technique later on.

Bargain Sources

There are many ways to obtain stone inexpensively, and in some cases there is no charge at all. If you are looking for rubblestone or fieldstone materials, you sometimes can obtain it for the price of hauling. Check first at road and building construction sites. In many instances, rock that must be removed for a building project has to be trucked away by the contractor, and you can get the stone for free (if you have the equipment to take it). Rubblestone also can be found around demolition sites. Many older homes utilized rubblestone, cut stone and fieldstone foundations; quite often you can obtain these materials in the same way. In most cases there will be some mortar adhered to the stones, but usually it is easy to scrub the mortar off. Wear gloves and goggles, and if necessary use a brick chisel.

In some parts of the country, local farmers are an excellent source for stones. Quite often, they will have outcroppings of stones or piles of stones that have been picked up from the fields. They may gladly sell, or you could offer to pick up the stones and cart them off the fields at no charge.

Selecting the Best Stones

When selecting natural stones, or any stones for that matter, try to pick only those that have flat, square sides. It almost is impossible to build anything with round, cannonball-shaped stones, although they can be inserted in mortared walls for an unusual design.

Naturally, the project will go faster if you use large stones. However, do not pick stones that are so large they dominate the project and look out of place. Large stones are hard to handle and hard to move. The weight of a stone will fool you. In most cases, stones of 40 or 50 pounds are not only difficult to lift, but they also make it much harder to construct the project properly. Stones weighing 15 to 25 pounds at the most provide a satisfying job in terms of design and construction.

When selecting natural stone for fieldstone projects, you will need at least 50 percent more than the total cubic volume of the project on

Quality of Stones

There are three basic qualities of stones: undressed, semidressed and dressed. Each is available at different price ranges; undressed stones are the least expensive—dressed are most expensive.

account of the wastage of stones that just will not fit. In fact, the more stones you can have on hand, the easier the job, because you can choose the stones you need from a wider selection. You also should have a good variety of sizes and shapes when doing natural fieldstone projects. The small stones fill in around the larger stones, providing the best design and construction.

Transporting the Stones

It does not take many stones to add up to a ton. The best choice for transporting the stones is a small rented trailer or a pick-up truck. Do not attempt to do this with your car. The weight is too much for the trunk of the car, and removing stones from the car is not good for your back. Use the first load as a test to see how much you should attempt to haul at one time. Be sure the truck's tires are properly inflated.

Sorting the Stones

Once you have a huge pile of stones in your back yard, separate them into piles. Sort out the best paving stones, which are the larger and flatter stones. They should have a straight

edge and sides. Then find other smaller stones that have straight edges and sides for filling the gaps between the large stones. Lay each of the stones out separately and flat on the ground so you can immediately survey the stone pile to find the exact stone size and shape you need. Leave about 4 to 6 feet of space between the stone pile and the proposed walk or patio, so you have room to work.

Laying Stone

On Sand. The thickness of individual stones varies, but when laying flagstone on sand, the stone must be at least 2 inches thick. Flagstone has uneven edges that create larger joints, which may make flagstone on a sand bed a nuisance unless the joints are filled with mortar (sand will not stay within wide joints). Mortared joints for flagstone are handled the same as for brick (see page 50). The stones are cut the same way other masonry is cut.

On the Ground or Over Sand-and-Gravel Base. Flagstone can be laid directly on the ground and this is often done for walks where a highly uniform surface is not required.

For areas subject to frost heave or where people will congregate, a more substantial base is necessary.

Excavate enough soil to permit you to install 4 inches of gravel, and 2 inches of sand underneath the stone. Plan carefully so that the finished stone surface will reach to the elevation you desire. Before you lay the gravel, level the soil well and tamp it with a hand tamper. Then, level and tamp the gravel.

On Concrete or Other Surfaces. You can lay flagstone on any surface that you can lay brick or other pavers. Stones thinner than 2 inches can be used on concrete. Check that the flagstone is correctly laid out before you fill the joints with mortar.

Using Ground Cover. As an alternative to mortar, you can use wider joints and extra soil. Plant a hardy ground cover between the stones. Most ground covers would not grow in the joints if the stones were laid over concrete, however the ground cover solution would work for flagstone laid over earth or for a 2-inch bed of sand with an earth base and sandy-earth joints.

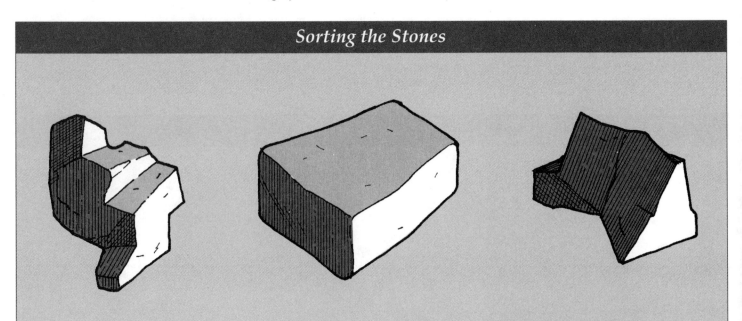

Sorting the Stones

Once you have the stones, sort them into separate piles. The larger stones are the best for building. Separate stones that have the straightest edges.

Cutting Stones

Cutting stone is not particularly hard, but it does take practice. Plan on wasting several pieces before you learn the process. You will need a stone mason's chisel, heavy, short-handled sledge, a pair of heavy-duty leather gloves and a pair of goggles.

1 **Scoring the Stone.** Position the stone on a solid spot on the ground. Mark a line with a piece of chalk where you wish to make the cut. Then hold the chisel in place on the line and lightly tap it with the hammer. As you tap, move the chisel along to score the marked line. Turn the stone over and do the same thing on the other side.

2 **Breaking the Stone.** In most instances, the stone will break along the second scored line as you tap it. If the stone does not break, turn it back over and continue tapping on the first side, deepening the groove until the stone breaks. Do not hit the chisel too hard. The trick is to hit it just hard enough to slightly score the stone.This takes practice, but once you get the hang of it you will be surprised at how easy it is.

In some cases, the stone just will not break. In other instances the stone may break, but not exactly where you want it to. In the latter case, do not worry too much; you can always use the smaller stones to fill in around the larger ones.

1 For those stones that must be cut, use a brick hammer and chisel to score the stone carefully.

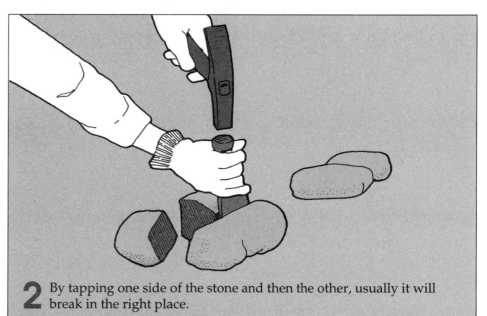

2 By tapping one side of the stone and then the other, usually it will break in the right place.

Cutting a Slab

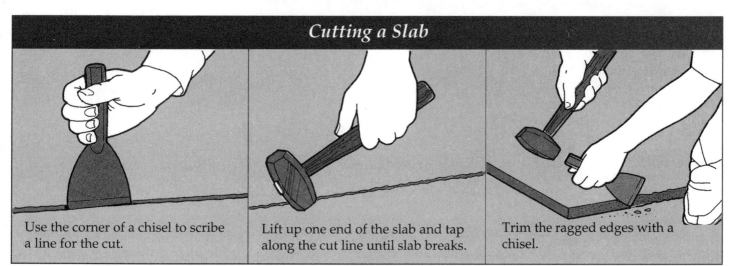

Use the corner of a chisel to scribe a line for the cut.

Lift up one end of the slab and tap along the cut line until slab breaks.

Trim the ragged edges with a chisel.

Laying Stone in Turf

There are two basic dry-laying construction systems. The first calls for cutting away the turf and dropping the stones individually in place, leaving the turf between the stones as part of the design. The second method involves laying the stones in a bed of sand, then filling in between the joints with sand.

A garden walk is an easy project, yet one that can add a great deal of beauty and practicality to a backyard or garden with little expense and effort. The walkway can be laid in a formal pattern using cut flagstones or a more informal pattern made of fieldstone.

Choose the stones you will use for this project. Naturally, they should be as flat as possible. So they will not crack or break, the stones used for this type of project must be at least 2 inches thick. You may wish to use cut stones such as flagstone or carefully selected, flat fieldstones.

1 Outlining the Walk. Lay out the outline of the sides of the walk. It can be curved, straight or angled. Place small stakes and connect strings to indicate the sides of the walk on the ground. It is a good idea to mow the grass down so it will be easier to work in the area. In most instances, the walk should be no less than 2 feet and no more than 3 feet wide.

2 Placing the Stones. If you are laying the stones individually in place in the turf, then merely lay one of the stones in place at one end and against the string line. Cut around it down below the sod, using a shovel with a sharp blade. Keep this sod nearby; you may need some of it later on for filling in around the stones.

3 Cutting the Sod. Lift up the stone, set it aside and dig out the area where the stone will be placed. Place the stone back in position and check to make sure that it is fairly level and that it does not rock back and forth. If it does, remove the stone

and dig out enough dirt to allow the stone to set level and solid. The stone should end up about 1 1/2 inches above ground level.

4 Setting the Stones. When you have the stone set in place to your satisfaction, position the second stone in the same manner and place it solidly in position. Leave a bit of sod between the two if possible, but if not you can tamp dirt back in place

between the stones later and then reseed the lawn. Before replacing dirt in a deep hole, add a layer of sand.

After the last stone has been placed, remove the stakes and strings and place sod around any areas that need it. You may have to place a little fill soil around each of the stones. This should be left somewhat high, as it will settle with time, if necessary.

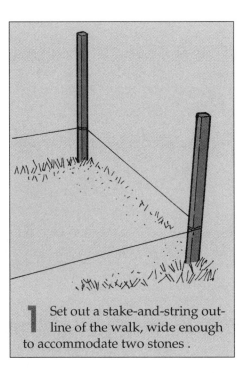

1 Set out a stake-and-string outline of the walk, wide enough to accommodate two stones .

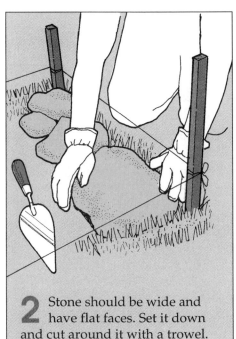

2 Stone should be wide and have flat faces. Set it down and cut around it with a trowel.

3 Cut away sod with a shovel. Excavate enough dirt so the top of the stone is at ground level.

4 Set the stone to sit securely. If it rocks, cut away more dirt until it sits steady.

Laying Stone on Sand

Another dry method of laying a walk or patio is to lay the stones on a bed or sand. This often provides a smoother, flatter, more even surface. It does, however, require more work.

You will need a shovel, raking board, broom and a carpenter's level.

1 Outlining the Project. For both a walk and a patio, the first step is to create the outline of the project using stakes and string.

2 Excavating. Use a shovel to remove all sod from the area. You will need to dig 2 inches deeper than the thickness of the stone to allow for a layer of sand to be placed under the stones. Keep the sod aside—you will need to fill in around the edges of the project and up against the rocks.

Try to cut the borders of the project as neatly as possible. An excellent way to create neat borders, as well as to add an unusual look, is to place redwood 2x4s as guide strips for the edging for the borders. These must be held in place with concealed stakes driven into the ground and nailed to the posts. These stakes are then covered over with sand. In most instances the 2x4s will provide just about the right depth for the 2-inch layer of sand and a 2-inch-thick stone surface, allowing the surface of the walk or patio to protrude above ground level about 1/2 inch.

Dig down to the correct depth and level the bottom so it is as smooth as possible. Remove any large roots or gravel.

3 Adding the Sand. Place a 2-inch layer of sand in the bottom. Rake it flat and smooth. A leveling board can be made to help even out the sand and make sure it does not have any high or low spots. Shape the sand so it is higher in the center than at the edges to help drain water away from the walk. The pitch should be very slight—about 1/8 inch per foot. After you have leveled out the sand with the board and rake, sprinkle the sand bed with water to pack it and provide a more solid surface.

4 Setting the Stone. Start placing the stones, working from one corner and against one string line. Space the stones with about 1 inch between them. Just as before, make sure they are solidly placed and won't wobble on a high area. If they do, remove them and dig away a bit of sand until the rocks are flat and evenly placed. Try to keep them placed as level as possible, using a long carpenter's level frequently to check their placement. Due to the nature of the stones, the level can't be exact, but do the best you can.

5 Filling in the Joints. Once all the stones have been positioned, sprinkle sand in the spaces in between joints. Fill all the joints well. Dampen the joints lightly. Wait a while and then sweep in more sand. Finally, lightly sweep excess sand from the surface. Use the sod you set aside to fill in all edges until they are as smooth and even as possible. To allow for settling, the soil should stand a little higher than the stones at this time.

Mortaring the Joints

You can place mortar in a sand-bed patio if you wish, but the mortar joints will crack and will not appear as neat as sand-filled joints. If you do decide to mortar the joints, make up a dry mix of about 1 part cement to 4 parts sand. Use this instead of the sand. Place the dry mortar-sand mix in and around the stones. After making sure you have all joints packed with the dry mortar, use a garden hose set on fine spray to dampen the mortar. Gently soak the joints, but do not flush any of the mortar away with the pressure of the water.

Setting Stones in Sand

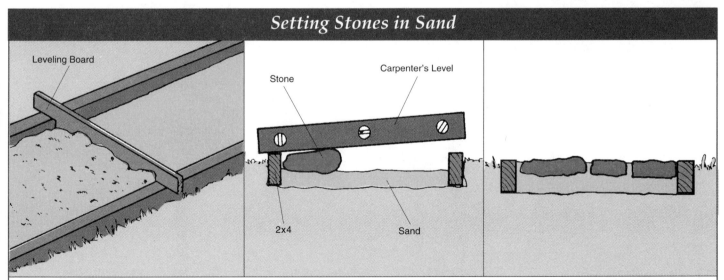

Leveling Board

Stone Carpenter's Level

2x4 Sand

To set stones in sand, excavate deep enough to allow for the stone plus the sand (left). Level the sand; then create as level a walking surface as you can (middle). Fill the joints with more sand (right).

Laying Stone in Mortar

To minimize any heaving in cold weather, it is recommended that stone be set in a bed of mortar over a clean, solid and well drained concrete surface (see pages 29-42). In fact, this is one way to refurbish an old concrete patio. Because the material is not uniform in shape and texture, it requires a little more planning in the beginning, primarily in planning a layout.

Lay out the project without mortar so you can determine the best arrangement. Use a nail to cut scratches into the concrete footing to indicate stone positions. Use a crayon or chalk to mark final locations for the stones.

Lay as many full stones as possible, in the pattern chosen. Use thin wooden strips as spacers to allow for the size of the mortar joints. Note the size of the closure stone. If possible, modify your plan so that the closure stone will be a full unit and cutting will not be necessary.

Stone absorbs moisture and unless it is wetted down before it is laid, it will suck the moisture out of the mortar. If a joint dries too rapidly, the mortar is weakened and does not properly adhere the stones. The stones do not need to be soaked. If they are dripping wet when they are laid the mortar mix may become to wet.

1 Preparing the Mortar Base. Prepare a standard mortar mix, lay and screed a 1/2-inch mortar bed. The procedure is similar to screeding sand (see page 38). Screed only a small, 3 square foot section at one time. Never mix more mortar than you can use in one hour.

2 Placing the Stone. Lay the stones in the mortar following the pattern you planned. Position and tap each stone firmly to avoid air pockets. Leave a minimum 1/2-inch-wide mortar joint between each stone and between the courses. The joints between the stones should be kept as small as possible in order to reduce the total area covered by joints. If too many joints occur, crevassing or dips between stones could cause a very uneven and imperfect wearing surface. Use a level and a long straightedge to ensure that all stones are level—high or low spots will cause water pooling. Make sure there are no air pockets trapped in the mortar below the stones; frost will cause stones to heave in the area around an empty air pocket.

3 Filling the Joints. You can trowel the joints flush with the stones or tool the joints slightly. Tooled joints, however, should not be made too deep, or the surface will be hard to keep clean.

Position the mortar near at hand so you do not have to reach very far for it. If you cannot get the wheelbarrow close enough to the job, use a mortar hawk and holder to hold a smaller amount close at hand.

■ Turn the trowel sideways 90 degrees so the blade is straight up and down.

■ At the same time, give a slightly downward flip of the trowel.

When the mortar is thrown or flung in this manner, the mortar adheres well to the surface and settles down deep into any depressions.

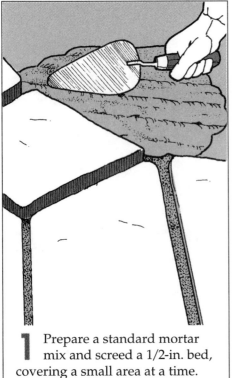

1 Prepare a standard mortar mix and screed a 1/2-in. bed, covering a small area at a time.

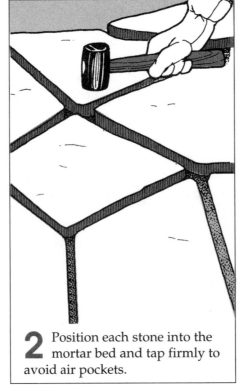

2 Position each stone into the mortar bed and tap firmly to avoid air pockets.

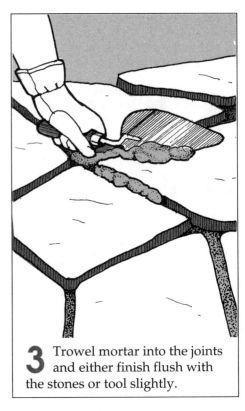

3 Trowel mortar into the joints and either finish flush with the stones or tool slightly.

OTHER PAVING MATERIALS

When it comes to paving materials, the choices reach far beyond the common brick and stone. Before deciding upon a paving material be sure to consider concrete patio block, interlocking pavers, wood and asphalt paving and modular paving. Each provides its own unique style and texture.

Concrete Patio Blocks

Concrete patio blocks come in a variety of sizes but the standard is 1 foot x 1 foot x 1 inch (1 square foot). Like other concrete blocks, patio blocks are relatively inexpensive. The blocks may be laid in a basket weave, running bond or any pattern you desire. They can be laid like any other stone, depending on their use. Whether they are utilized for rough walks through natural surroundings or smooth finish walks and terraces close to the house, your purpose and your climate will determine the type joint and the method of installation.

Calculating how many blocks are needed is no real problem. It is always best to order some extra blocks. Since patio blocks (as well as bricks) must be cut to fill in at the edges, there is a chance that some of the blocks may be broken incorrectly and will need replacing. Blocks also may crack under stress or in severe weather. You should have at least 20 extra blocks on hand for these situations.

1 **Removing Soil.** Some guide books will tell you to dig out enough soil for a 2-inch bed of sand beneath your blocks. In a hard frost area, this is not enough. You will need to dig out at least 4 inches below the bottom of the block. For proper drainage, a block patio should drop 2 inches for every 10 feet. A 10-foot-square patio, for example, would be 2 inches lower at one end than at the other. If you are using standard, 1-inch-thick patio blocks, you would need to remove 5 inches of soil at the highest point and 7 inches in the lowest. Measure the boundaries of your patio and set up edger boards and corner stakes, using the same methods as for the brick patio. The ideal base for a block patio consists of 2 inches of fine limestone gravel (called "tailings" or "traffic mix") at the very bottom of the patio bed.

2 **Laying the Base.** To lay the actual base for the blocks, you will need 2 inches of sharp sand. Note that the correct type of sand for a base is torpedo sand–not the finer, mason's sand used in mortar mixes. When spread evenly, the torpedo sand provides excellent drainage and will stay in place. Finer sands tend to wash away or shift in heavy rains. Add the layer of sand, following along the top of the edger board, which follows the slope that you set when removing the soil. This will achieve your grade for drainage.

3 **Placing the Blocks.** By measuring from the top of the edger board to the top of the sand, you will have a space 1 inch from the top of the sand for the blocks. The top of the edger board will indicate the position of each block as you move along. You should periodically recheck the grade with a carpenter's level. Begin placement in a corner, working from the highest point to lowest. Check frequently for correct grade.

4 **Filling the Joints.** When all the blocks are in place, carefully sweep mason's sand (the fine type) into the joints between the blocks. Wet the sand thoroughly and let dry. Then spread more sand across the blocks, sweep, wet and let dry. For added strength, mix the sand with portland cement on a 1:1 ratio and sweep into the joints. Wet and let dry for two or three days before using the patio.

You may wish to finish off the edges of the patio by either using sod, railroad ties or heavy blocks to keep the edges in place. For 1½-inch-thick end blocks, build a mold out of two 5-foot 2x4s nailed to a 2x6 or 2x8. Caulk the joints carefully with any ordinary household caulk, and oil the mold with motor oil. Next, mix a bag of mortar, pour it into the mold and let dry for 10 hours. Remove the end block from the mold and let cure for 3 days before setting in place.

1 Dig out at least 4 in. below the bottom of the block.

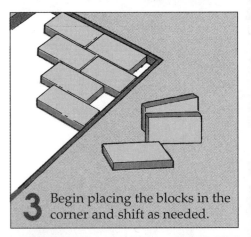

2 Use torpedo sand when laying the base for blocks.

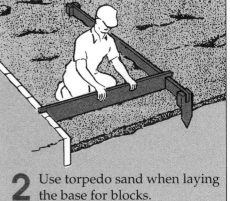

3 Begin placing the blocks in the corner and shift as needed.

4 Sweep mason's sand into the joints between the blocks.

Interlocking Pavers

Interlocking pavers are another concrete product, with a wide variety of shapes, such as double hex units, curvilinear units, and other patterns. All of them interlock or interconnect naturally because of their shape. The interlocking pavers require the same installation techniques as regular concrete pavers. Where the soil and climate permit, pavers may be laid right on the ground. As with most concrete blocks, they are relatively inexpensive.

Choosing a Base

Over Concrete. Pavers may be laid over a concrete slab. When this method is used and the joints are mortared and finished with a joint tool, the surface has a smooth, highly finished appearance with a line value similar to that of a brick surface.

Over Sand. Pavers on a base of sand can have either sand or mortar joints. If sand joints are chosen, note that concrete pavers are good in areas where there are trees. The pavers lift up when the tree roots grow, rather than break and crack as would a concrete slab. Concrete pavers with sand joints also allow drainage down to the roots of the trees and shrubs.

Design & Strength

Patterns and Joints. Concrete pavers can be laid with closed joints (each paver butted against the other with no joints). Pavers may be grouped within wooden grids in the same manner as poured concrete. They may be laid in basket weave, ashlar, grid, running bond, or nearly any pattern you need. Usage, climate and soil conditions will determine the best type of joint and the preferred method of installation.

Installation. Pavers are split in the same manner as common brick. However, their installation is a little different than that of other materials.

Interlocking Pavers. To install pavers, begin at lower left corner and work clockwise around the patio. Use the pavers as a surface from which to work as you lay the units.

Excavate 4 inches for the gravel and sand, plus the depth of the paver plus 2 inches all the way across to allow for grade. Add the gravel layer. Then spread a base of torpedo sand at least 2 inches thick across the entire patio area. Check the grade in the sand using a level and a long, straight 2x4. If you need to adjust the grade, add more sand. Once the grade is set, do not step back on the sand. If you must step on the sand again, regrade it. Tamp the sand thoroughly.

Starting from a corner, lay four or five pavers in line and work straght to the next corner, standing only on the blocks you have laid, and not on the sand (see above).

When complete, sweep fine mason's sand onto the paving stones and wet the sand. The pavers will interlock to form a continuous, firm surface. Repeat this process.When the patio is done, finish the edges with railroad ties or end blocks. Some paver manufacturers make special end stones for this purpose.

Finally, sweep the patio well, wash it down with a garden hose and apply a coat of cement sealer to extend the patio's life.

For each square foot, you will need $2\frac{1}{2}$ pavers, depending on their shape. For example, a 10x10-foot patio would require 250 stones.

Wood Paving

Pressure-treating techniques have made wood a durable, versatile, relatively cheap and easy-to-install pavement. Pressure-treated wood may be installed below ground, on grade, or raised to allow the existing drainage to remain essentially unaltered.

Treated Wood Specifications.

Pressure-treated wood is available in all sizes, enabling a wide range of paving designs. There are established standards for wood treatment quality. Treated wood should be stamped with proper usage information. Pieces marked LP-22 ABOVE GROUND USE ONLY .25 should be used only where the wood will not be in direct contact with the earth, as for walks on stringers above ground. Pieces marked LP-22 GROUND CONTACT .40 may be used for on-ground projects and some in-ground projects, such as fence posts. FDN FOUNDATION .60 means the wood is suitable for use completely underground—in some cases, even in building foundation work. The decimal figure indicates the amount of treatment per unit area of wood.

Using Treated Wood. The timbers can be laid on gravel or sand and staked at the outside timber. Installing a 1 x 3 spacer at regular intervals—about 4 feet on center—helps keep the timber exactly parallel as you install it.

For another variation, lay stringers on a gravel bed and nail 4x6 timbers across them. In this case, stringers are sections of 4x6 running the length of the walk. They should be set into the gravel about 2 inches to secure the walk in position while supporting the cross members. This is a slightly raised walk.

For a more static appearance, the same timbers may be cut into 4-inch sections and laid in a bed of sand much the same as for brick on sand. As for all pavements laid in sand, add a permanent border.

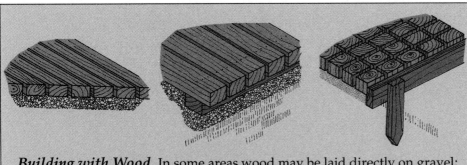

Building with Wood. In some areas wood may be laid directly on gravel; sturdier patios and walks are nailed to stringers—parallel or perpendicular to the walk or patio; timber sections may be set in sand.

Asphalt Paving

Everyone is accustomed to asphalt streets and driveways as they are a utilitarian necessity. However, as a low-cost design material, asphalt has not realized its full potential. In many instances asphalt can do the same job that concrete does, at a lower cost. It also is one of the easiest to install.

Asphalt is an ideal material for paths and walkways. Just lay it and let it weather. If you do not like the black color, a colored topping, such as gravel or crushed brick can be rolled onto the surface. You can cover whole areas with it, or you can combine it with walks of other materials such as concrete and brick. Use asphalt for the surrounding areas and walks to more secluded, less-visible areas. Specially manufactured asphalt paints are available in a range of colors to contrast or blend the asphalt with the surroundings.

Hot Asphalt. Hot asphalt, also called asphalt concrete, is made by coating crushed rock with hot asphalt cement. It bonds much as concrete does. This is the kind of asphalt you see when the city repaves a street. Paving contractors use special equipment to compact the rock and spray the hot asphalt. It is difficult work, and is not for the amateur. Unless you have some special condition that requires hot asphalt, you probably could not justify the extra cost of using it. If you would like to use it, hire a contractor.

Cold Asphalt. Cold asphalt can be bought in a premixed form. It is spread out and then tamped or rolled in place. A do-it-yourselfer can handle this job.

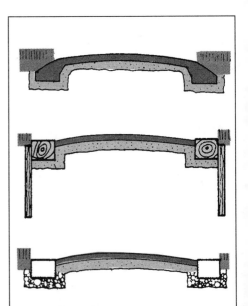

Building with Asphalt. Asphalt is an excellant material for walks and patios; however, the edges must be reinforced or they will break down quickly. Edges can be thickened asphalt (top), railroad ties (middle) or concrete block (bottom).

Building Modular Paving

One of the simplest and most versatile paving units is a 2x2-foot wood module that can be assembled as a walk, or just about any outdoor area. The wood should be pressure-treated. The following describes the building procedure and gives material requirements for a 4-foot-wide walk that is 36 feet long.

Tools and Materials. You need a pencil and a carpenter's ruler, a hand or power saw and a hammer. Each block is made from two 8-foot lengths of 2x4 lumber and 24 8d galvanized nails; the galvanizing resists rust. For this walk size you need 36 2x2-foot modules.

To prepare the ground for the 36 feet of walk, you will need a shovel, garden rake, six 80-pound bags of sand, 144 square feet of 6 ml black polyethylene, four 2-foot stakes, some string and four 12-foot 2x6s.

Assembling the Modules. From each piece of 2x4 cut three pieces 1 foot, 11½ inches long for top boards, and one piece 2 feet long for a stringer. You will have a total of 6 top boards and 2 stringers from both 2x4s. Lay the top pieces on the two stringers; space them evenly, allowing 1/4 inch on the sides and ends of the runners.

Use four 8d nails, two on each end, to attach each top board to the bottom stringer. You may nail from the top or bottom depending on whether you want the nails to show. Install the nails at least one inch in from the ends and sides of the lumber to avoid splitting the timber. For easier nailing, holes may be pre-drilled using a 3/32-inch drill bit. The modules can be built inside the house, or outdoors, and stored in the garage or basement until it is convenient to lay the walk. With blocks this size, almost any job goes quickly.

Installing Modular Units

Preparing the Base. Prepare the walk area by pounding 2-foot stakes into the ground to mark each corner and by running string between stakes to outline the walk. Remove the topsoil to a minimum depth of 4 inches and smooth the surface with the rake. Lay a 2-inch base of compacted sand in the excavated area. Install the perimeter 2x6s set on edge, butted together at the corners and nailed at each end with two 8d nails.

Cover the sand or gravel with 6 ml polyethylene film to eliminate weed growth and then cover the film with a 2-inch base of sand. The black polyethylene will not be noticeable. Use a heavy nail or rod 1/4 inch in diameter to punch drainage holes about 12 inches on center across the surface.

Setting the Modules. Level the sand with a rake. Start placing the modules, working from a corner. Butt each one snugly to the next. After the modules are in position with the walk perimeter, backfill around the edges of the walk to create a smooth transition from the lawn to the walk.

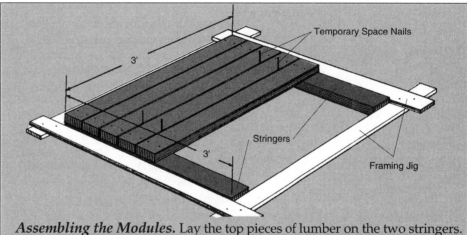

Assembling the Modules. Lay the top pieces of lumber on the two stringers. Spacing them evenly, allow 1/4" on the sides and ends of the runners.

Preparing the Base. Remove the topsoil to a minimum depth of 4" and smooth with a rake. Then, lay a base of compacted sand.

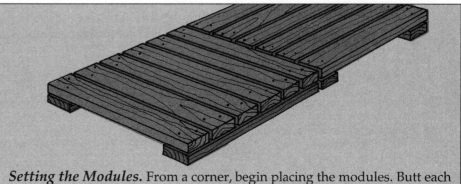

Setting the Modules. From a corner, begin placing the modules. Butt each one snugly to the next.

Loose Paving

While these materials involve maintenance problems, they have certain qualities that may make them very attractive. These natural materials create their own surface textures. The textures will appear different in different light situations. Generally, gravel, bark and chips provide good drainage. They are quick and inexpensive to install.

Loose paving requires sturdy edgings or the material will spread. Concrete, wood, or brick can be used. Provided that your edging has reasonable flexibility, your walk can curve, change shape and be any width you desire.

Warning. Children tend to look at these loose fill materials as a limitless sand pile substitute. You may find that, having carefully laid out your walk, installed the edgings, and raked the material smooth, your efforts are rewarded by a child who has pushed whole areas into a giant "road-building" project with a toy truck.

Maintenance. These patios and walks require annual, or more frequent, renewal. Once your landscaping has been completed, there may be no way for a truck to get near your path in order to replenish the walk. You may face the prospect of pushing many wheelbarrow loads of gravel or bark to your walk and then raking the surface smooth.

Gravel

Gravel is an inexpensive material used for walks. It comes in many sizes and colors. There are two types: pea gravel (natural or rounded), and crushed stone or rock.

When used as a patio or walk, gravel needs raking almost daily. Gravel scatters easily and tends to be carried away in heavy rains. It also may sink into the earth and require annual replenishment.

Gravel does not absorb water as do organic materials and thus is a good drainage material.

Size and Shape. Gravel is available crushed or whole in various sizes. The crushed gravel is typically 1/4 to 3/4 inch—although it can be found in much larger pieces or stones. Crushed aggregate is usually not a good walking surface because the edges of the crushed material are sharp on barefeet. However, it acts as a good drainage base. Whole gravel is available in nearly round form and in smooth, irregular forms, ranging from 1/4 to 2 inch and larger to stone sizes. The larger pieces are not comfortable to walk on but are good for decorative purposes such as a cobble-like edging. Crushed or whole, gravel packs best when there is a mix of sizes from about 1/4 to 1 inch. This mix will compact into a comfortable surface for walking. Uniform sizes do not pack well, and will move around when walked on.

Bark & Wood Chips

Bark blends in well with natural surroundings. In kitchen gardens, the bark becomes a useful mulch as it decomposes. The old bark, when decayed, can be transferred to the compost pile and replaced with new bark. It is a good way to obtain paths and mulch at the same time.

Fir bark is a warm, dark bark that does not splinter readily. Therefore, it is an excellent material to use in children's play areas—around swings, slides, etc. It will last as long as three years with a little maintenance. The soil beneath may be sterilized if you wish, in order to cut down on weeding. When using loose materials, however, it is probably best to avoid soil sterilizers and to simply pluck the weeds that come through.

Constructing Loose Paving

Patios of loose paving are the easiest to construct. The base preparation is minimal. Excavate about 6 1/2 inches and prepare the soil base as previously described. The gravel for the patio should be contained within a metal or wood edging strip, which can be placed in the excavated area. Once the area has been prepared and the soil base has been tamped, place river-washed or peastone gravel in the forms; a depth of 4 inches is recommended. The gravel should be a little lower than the edging so it does not spill over.

Creating Edges. Loose paving creates its own surface texture, depending upon material used. Edgings are a must.

EDGINGS FOR PATIOS & WALKS

Any paved surface will last longer and look better if its edges are protected. Unprotected edges eventually will crumble and fall apart. The methods and materials discussed here can be used to contain any of various paving surfaces used for patios and walks.

Building Edgings

The main requirement of any edging scheme is that it contain the material of the walk. Concrete needs no special edging unless a concentrated load is likely to be placed at the edge. For example, if the walk is placed so that an automobile will be driven frequently over the edge.

The need for edging is less apparent with a material like asphalt or brick than it is for loose materials such as bark or gravel. Any surface, however, will last longer and look better if you protect its edges, which gradually would crumble and fall off otherwise. The methods discussed here can be used to contain various patio and walk materials.

Railroad Ties

Another way to protect asphalt surfaces is to add a continuous edge made of railroad ties. Both the surface and the ties rest on a 4-inch base of gravel or sand. Hold the cross ties firmly in place with pressure-treated 2x4 stakes. Drive the stakes flush against the cross ties to a depth of about 2 feet. Then nail them to the cross ties with galvanized nails. For 8-foot railroad ties, use a stake at each end and one in the middle of each tie.

Landscape Timbers

Another way to protect patios and walks is to make an edge out of a pressure-treated 2x6 landscaping timber. The 2x6 is staked like the cross tie curb described on page 68. The edge rests on a 4-inch bed of sand. This is probably the least effective of the edges described here. But, where it is desirable to have a less prominent edge for aesthetic reasons, or where your budget does not allow a more substantial method, this curb will suffice.

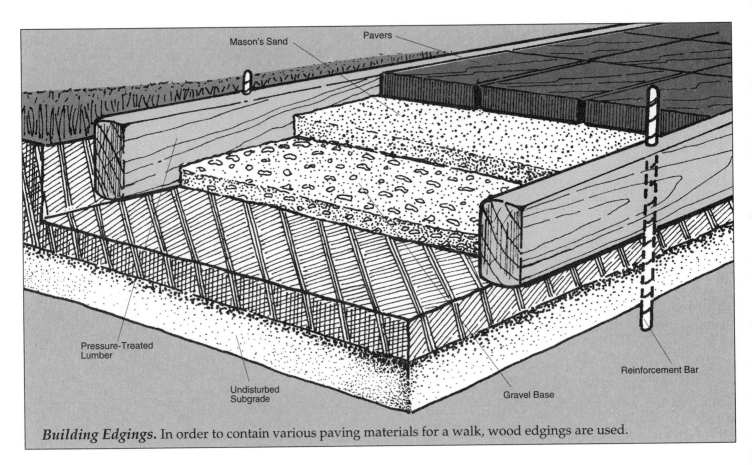

Building Edgings. In order to contain various paving materials for a walk, wood edgings are used.

Brick or Concrete Block

An edge of bricks or concrete block can be constructed by standing them on end, directly in the ground. Simply dig a narrow trench around the perimeter of the planned patio or walk. The trench should be deep enough to cover half or more of the height of the brick or block. Position the bricks or blocks in the trench, level the tops and pack the soil around the outside.

To provide a more stable base for the bricks, pour a footing of concrete into the trench before positioning the bricks.

Stone

Flagstone, cobblestones and small boulders can be used to edge a patio or very wide walk. Flagstone and cobblestone are best set on a concrete base. Boulders can either be set in concrete or set directly in the soil.

Concrete

Surfaces also can be protected with a concrete curb. The curb requires form work. A concrete curb 8 inches wide and 1 foot deep should be adequate for most localities—check local building codes. Lay a concrete curb on 4 inches of gravel. After the concrete has cured, the asphalt can be tamped over 4 inches of gravel or coarse sand. The curb will make the tamping easier and allow you to build a denser walk.

Asphalt

Asphalt walks and patios can be protected by thickening the edges and turning them down beneath the ground surface. A 4-inch asphalt patio could be protected by thickening the edges to 8 inches tall, and about 1 foot wide all around. Turning the edges under the soil prevents crumbling while thickening them provides extra strength and support.

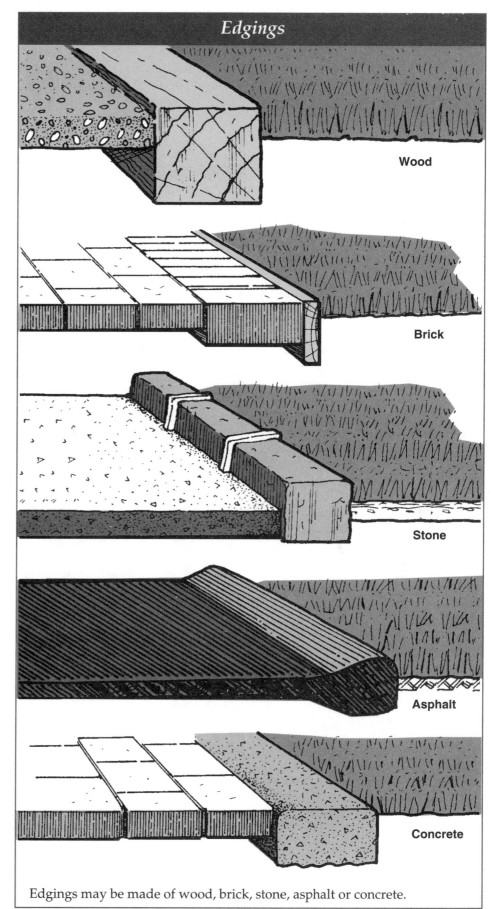

Wood

Brick

Stone

Asphalt

Concrete

Edgings may be made of wood, brick, stone, asphalt or concrete.

Special Support Base for Railroad Ties

Cross ties may be used for a grid, as an edging material, or as a permanent form for the sides and tread edges of steps. In each case a support base will be necessary to keep them level and dry. They are heavy and they will lay level if you merely smooth the earth beneath them, but they may gradually settle if the soil has not been compacted.

To prevent settling, you must compact the soil with a hand tamper and then lay down a 4-inch bed of gravel. The gravel will aid drainage and help combat frost heave.

When using concrete paving you must provide a way to keep the paving and ties on the same horizontal plane, while allowing space for the material to expand and contract. To do this, attach 1/2-inch diameter bolts that are 6 inches or longer to the side of the tie that will be in contact with the concrete. These bolts should be sunk into the tie, leaving 3 inches protruding from the tie. Space the bolts between 2 and 4 feet on center and place them continuously along the tie.

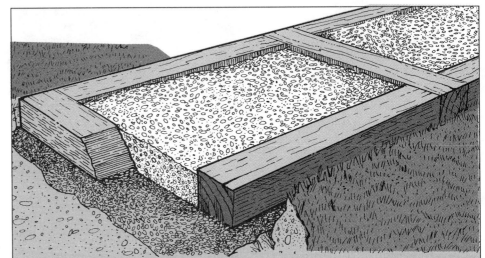

Loose Paving. Cross ties are sturdy edgings for loose pavings such as gravel or wood chips.

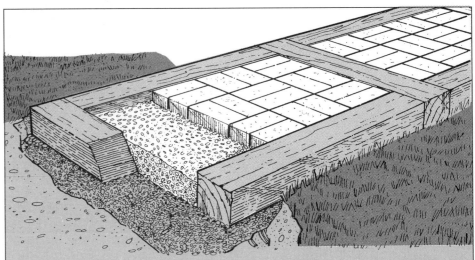

Brick. Cross ties are neat borders in which brick patterns can be tightly held in place.

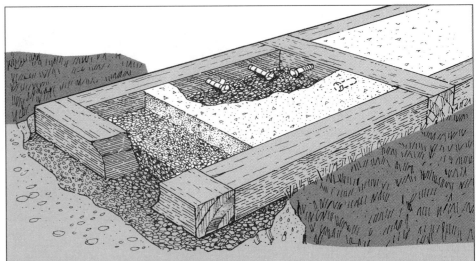

Concrete. In order to keep concrete paving and ties on the same horizontal plane, bolts are sunk into the ties.

STEPS, RAMPS & BRIDGES

The purpose of all steps and ramps is to allow the movement of people and equipment from one grade to another in safety and comfort. In addition to being very functional elements, steps and ramps can be visual assets to your total outdoor design.

Functional & Design Considerations

There are some very specific, technical requirements that pertain to the design and construction of steps and ramps. It is important that you understand these details before attempting to build. Before you begin determining riser heights or ramp slopes, consider the following:

■ What do I want these steps or ramps to do?

■ Who will use them?

■ How can I make the steps and ramps contribute to the total design?

Dealing with Slopes

Evaluating Options

If you keep the major questions in mind, the technical solutions will fall into place. For example, there is no set width for steps, and no "best" material. The primary requirement is that the steps work for you and look right for your project. If you have a big house and plan extensive outdoor entertaining on a large, multilevel patio or in the yard, a single, 4-foot-wide flight of steps between levels will not do the job—functionally or aesthetically. In this case, steps that extend the entire length of the patio (or several separate steps) would work and look better. Depending on circumstances and the grading, however, you may actually need a ramp rather than steps. A gentle slope would not require steps.

Ramps. Ramps perform the same function as steps, but if you or a guest happens to be in a wheelchair, any flight of steps is not a comforting sight. If your slope must be climbed by people in wheelchairs or with canes, children on bicycles and tricycles, or anyone using wheeled lawn equipment, you may find that a ramp is a more feasible option. Some circumstances may require a combination of ramps and steps.

Proportions and Size. A large house with a wide patio calls for steps and/or ramps on a similar scale. However, if you have a small, intimate patio right outside a bedroom, wide steps would look ridiculous. Study your needs and the scale of the surroundings carefully before you begin designing steps and ramps.

Design Guidelines

People designing for typical urban and suburban environments have found that certain guidelines on tread/riser relationships and ramp slope relationships can be very helpful. Here are some notes on tread/riser relationships.

■ Many experts believe that the best tread/riser proportion for the garden is a 15-inch tread with a 6-inch riser. This ratio is probably the most popular, but it cannot always be achieved, nor is it always appropriate for your needs.

■ If steps join a walk or are part of a walk, the steps should be the same width as the walk.

■ If possible, where a flight of steps abuts a walk or drive at a right angle, the steps should be set back at least 2 feet from the walk.

■ The tread/riser relationship should be consistent throughout the flight.

■ The treads should be pitched forward approximately 1/8 inch per foot to assure adequate drainage.

■ Landings should be the same width as the treads, and not less than 3 feet long.

■ Stair railings are recommended for flights in which the rise is greater than 30 inches.

■ Avoid risers that are less than 4 inches and more than 7 inches—for stepped ramps as well as flights of steps.

■ Avoid treads that are less than 11 inches deep.

■ Treads and risers should not be tapered. For example, if you have a 6-inch riser, it should be 6 inches along the entire width of the steps. The same is true for treads.

■ All sections of ramps falling between risers (treads) should be the same length.

Sizes mentioned above are commonly used relationships, even if not acknowledged standards. Variations from these relationships are uncommon and, therefore, unexpected. Changes from standard proportions could cause an accident. You should design on a larger scale for outdoor steps and walks and ramps than you would for inside steps. Small steps tend to look small and out of scale on generous suburban landscapes; but if you are designing for a small, intimate, urban lot, your step space may be at a premium. The basic requirement always remains the same: steps, ramps and walks must be wide enough to accommodate the traffic they will have to handle. A 4-foot garden walk usually is adequate for one person to stroll comfortably, but a walk that is 5 feet or greater is needed for two people. If at all possible, never

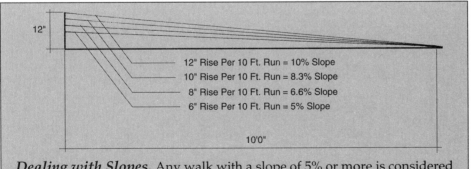

Dealing with Slopes. Any walk with a slope of 5% or more is considered a ramp. When the grade reaches a slope of more than 8.3%, a ramp must be combined with steps for comfortable walking.

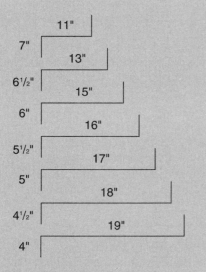

The relationship between treads and risers differs from what is logically expected; the higher the riser, the shallower the tread. Low risers have deeper treads.

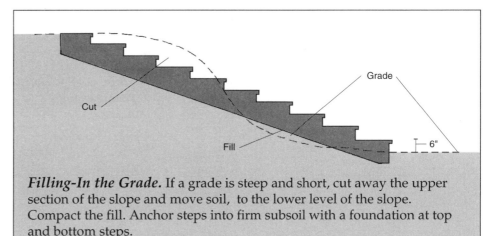

Filling-In the Grade. If a grade is steep and short, cut away the upper section of the slope and move soil, to the lower level of the slope. Compact the fill. Anchor steps into firm subsoil with a foundation at top and bottom steps.

reduce the width to less than 1 1/2 to 2 feet and then do so only for short lengths.

Figuring Step Requirements

Finding the Run and the Rise.

Insert a tall stake (Stake 1) into the ground at the point where the bottom riser will meet the ground. Pound in a second stake (Stake 2) at the highest point of the top riser. If the steps are to connect different ground levels, the second stake will be much shorter than the first. The tops of both should be about level.

Tie a string at ground level (or the landing level) onto Stake 2. Run the string over to Stake 1–check it with a level. Measure the length of the string. This is the total length of the steps' treads, or the run. On the bottom stake, measure the distance between the ground and the string. This distance equals the total height of the risers of the steps, or the rise.

Determining slope. To find the slope, divide the rise by the run. The slope will affect your plan. It is the angle of the steps. In a "normal" situation, such as steps connecting a house and a walk, the angle is about 45 degrees. If the angle is greater than 45 degrees, you may have to incorporate landings, create a series of diagonal paths for the steps, or cut away part of the slope to ease the angle.

In the last case, you may need retaining walls, a ground cover or a rock garden, to prevent soil erosion. If there is a portion of the site that is quite steep, while the majority of it is flat or gently sloping, you may again need a retaining wall. If the retaining wall is to hold a steep (3 feet or higher) vertical embankment, you should have a professional design and build it. Shorter or stepped-back walls of boulders or railroad ties are sufficient for slope control at heights of 3 feet or less.

If the slope is slight, you can incorporate landings or ramps between flights (the flights need be only one or two steps high).

When the slope or grade is steep, you have to change the layout of the steps or ramps to increase the amount of run relative to the rise of the slope. This means the route down the slope will not be straight. Another solution is that a flight of steps can be raised on stilts. A more complex solution might incorporate a series of landings that jog down the slope.

Filling-In the Grade. If necessary, the slope itself may be modified by cutting from the top and filling at the bottom (see above).

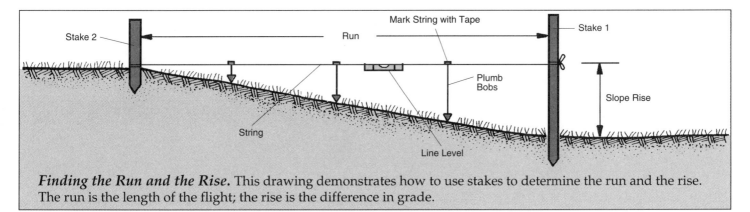

Finding the Run and the Rise. This drawing demonstrates how to use stakes to determine the run and the rise. The run is the length of the flight; the rise is the difference in grade.

Concrete Steps

To build the steps of concrete, follow the same design and layout procedures as for wooden steps. The framework of the wooden stringer steps can be used as the form for the concrete steps. Side braces are needed to support the form against the weight of the concrete.

If the soil base is firm, reinforcements may be eliminated, or wire mesh substituted for the rods. Check with your building department concerning safety codes and requirements.

Almost all steps should be placed on footings. Flights of more than five steps require a centered landing.

There should be a large, flat landing at the top of the stairs if it leads to the entrance of the house. It should be large enough to allow you to open a door outward without stepping down to a lower step.

Figuring the Rise, Run and Slope. Using the instructions found on page 71, determine the rise and the run. Then use this information to figure the slope, also described on page 71.

Tread and Riser Sizes. Treads and risers should relate to the average length of a person's stride. As a rule of thumb for exterior steps, the width of a tread and two risers together should equal 26 inches. The recommended height of the risers is 6 inches, and they should never be less than 3 inches or more than 7 inches. The best width for the treads is 12 to 14 inches—never less than 12 inches. Try to stay close to the ideal, for these ratios are what most people expect. Be careful that no step is oddly short or tall.

Following these proportions, if the height of the steps is equal 30 inches, you will need 5 risers of 6 inches each. A distance of 65 inches means that the tread will be 13 inches wide (65/5=13).

Footing Excavation. Because of their weight, steps require footings. First excavate to the depth required by code. This excavation should extend at least 1 1/2 feet beyond all sides of the outline of the steps providing room for forms and bracing.

You can install a footing form, pour the footing and allow it to set before you erect the forms for the steps, but more commonly the footings and steps are poured at once. As stated before, post hole footings are a good choice for steps. You will need two or more post holes with a diameter of from 6 to 8 inches beneath the location of the bottom tread. You will need two or more post holes with a diameter of from 6 to 8 inches beneath the location of the bottom tread.

Steps without Footings. If the steps run between the ground and a patio that has been constructed level with interior floors, follow the same forming instructions given below. These steps require no footings.

Creating Forms for Steps. Draw your plan to scale before you begin. Take the drawing along when you purchase the boards, so that you buy the correct size. To get boards for the risers that are 6 to 7 inches wide, a standard 2x8 will have to be "ripped," which is the term for making lengthwise cuts in stock lumber. Unless you are very experienced, do not attempt to rip lumber yourself; ask the supplier to do it for you.

Constructing the Forms. Construct the forms with braces. Move the tops of the riser boards outward so that they are angled by about 1 inch. The top edge of the riser supporting the front of a given tread should be about 1/8 to 1/4 inch higher than the bottom edge of the next riser behind the same tread. These dimensions provide a pitch for water drainage. Bevel the lower edges of each rise form board, with the high side of

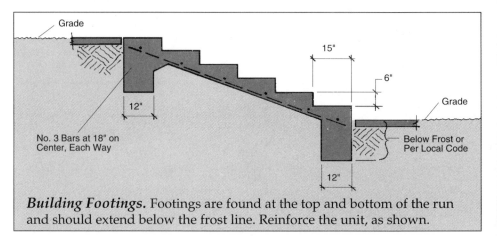

Building Wood Forms. Concrete steps are durable and can be built to almost any size. However, they require the construction of forms nearly as complete as a full set of wood steps.

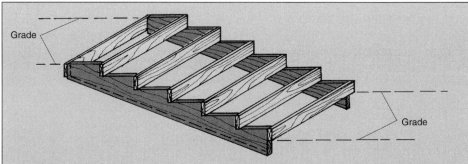

Building Footings. Footings are found at the top and bottom of the run and should extend below the frost line. Reinforce the unit, as shown.

bevel away from the pour. This permits room to float the steps. Because the weight of the concrete increases with its height, provide extra strong forming and braces for this project. Support the braces.

Making the Pour. Use gravel that is no more than 1 inch in diameter. Before beginning, insert two metal anchor bolts into the foundation wall of the house, below the location of either the top step or the landing. These will help tie the steps to the house and prevent shifting due to heaving and settling.

In the case of large-size steps, you can fill in some of the area with fairly large stones, but do not allow them to get near the sides of the forms or they will protrude through the finished sides. Tamp the stones securely in place.

Add an isolation joint between the house and the landing. Start with the bottom step. Pour, screed off the excess, and then pour the next step and screed it off level. Continue up to the landing. Tamp the concrete

securely down into all corners and around all edges to prevent the concrete from honey-combing with air pockets. When you have finished the pour, again screed off the

surface. This time, start with the top step or landing and work down, removing excess concrete as you go (see page 42).

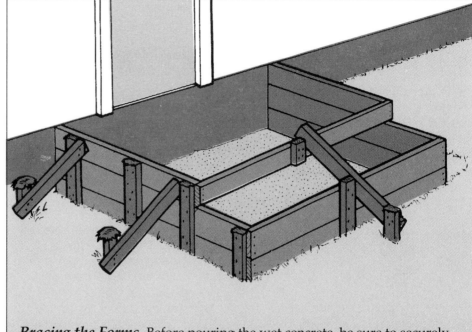

Bracing the Forms. Before pouring the wet concrete, be sure to securely brace the forms. Both the front and sides should be braced.

Building Steps with Brick

Brick, when used for steps, is probably best used as a veneer. Brick has no more strengths as a foundation material than cheaper materials. You can use brick with a wood framework as described below, or over concrete steps, or in some combination. The main appeal of brick as a step veneer is its warm appearance, variety of patterns and durability.

Laying Brick & Wood Steps

1. Compute the heights of the treads and risers. Remember to include the thickness of the brick when calculating the height of the riser. Plan the treads so that the space from front to back will be filled by two bricks, plus whatever joint you use; you will have to cut bricks.

2. Saw the notches on the 2x12 stringers, as discussed on page 76.

3. As an alternative to a concrete foundation, use 4x4 posts to secure the stringers. Set posts a minimum of 18 inches deep in a bed of gravel; then fill the hole to slightly above grade with concrete.

4. Lay the stringers on a 4-inch bed of gravel.

5. Nail the stringers to the foundation posts.

6. Nail 2x12 sidewalls to the stringers so that the bottom of the side wall is flush with the bottom of the stringer.

7. Nail the risers to the 2x12 stringers.

8. Fill the area within the stringers and sidewalls with gravel to provide a base on which to lay the brick.

9. Lay the brick treads even with the stringer notches on the gravel base and check regularly with a level.

10. Fill the joints with sand and tamp down.

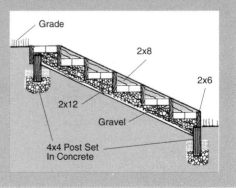

Wood Steps Built with Notched Stringers

This step-building technique calls for a 2x12 stringer notched to accommodate the treads and risers. If you work out a good drawing, you can prefabricate the steps and then set them in place. You also can build them on location and draw in the tread and riser notches on the stringers.

1 Determining Stringer Length.
Measure the slope along the ground to determine the length of the stringer material. If you were building steps down from a retaining wall, you could find the stringer length arithmetically: slope squared=run squared+rise squared. The slope in this example is just over 8 feet. Therefore, you must use the next standard board length, 10 feet, for your stringer. Cut the board to the length desired.

Another way to find the stringer lengths is to create a drawing to scale. Since it is recommended that you always work out an accurate drawing before starting any construction, this is a good way to begin.

2 Determining Riser Heights.
Measure the vertical difference in elevation that the steps must span and divide by 6 inches. For example, if the difference in elevation is 5 feet 1¼ inches, divide by 6 inches, to determine that you need ten 6⅛-inch risers. All risers should fall between 6 and 7 inches.

3 Determining Tread Depths.
Assume the run (horizontal length) of your slope is 11 feet, 5¼ inches. Dividing by 15 inches, each tread turns out to be 15¼ inches. The risers of 6⅛ inches and the treads of 15¼ inches are close to the ideal outdoor relationship of tread to riser, which is 6 inches for the riser and 15 inches for the tread.

4 Planning the Foundation.
Lay out your stringers to measure the treads and risers. Remove enough slope (or fill), then lay a base of 4 inches of gravel. The stringer should span the slope. Stringers may be notched to fit over a concrete foundation at the top and rest on a concrete foundation at the bottom. This is the preferred system. The foundation at the top can be a patio,

Wooden Steps Built with Support Cleats

You may want to build steps in which the treads mount between the stringers on 2x4 cleats, eliminating the 2x6 risers. This will give a more open, airy appearance to the steps. This method does not have as much strength in the steps as in notched stringers. The cleat blocks are nailed to the stringers under the ends of each tread. The remainder of the building process is the same as for the notched-stringer steps.

house foundation or retaining wall—whatever conveniently located feature exists—and the foundation at the bottom may be a walk, another patio or wall. Cross ties may be substituted for the lower foundation by recessing them in the ground on a bed of gravel. For the top foundation, the ties can be bolted to an existing structural member, and the stringers notched to fit as for concrete. In temperate climates (with no frost heave) you can use a concrete block foundation. Check local codes. Do not secure the stringers to the foundations at this time.

The type of foundation and the way the stringers meet and are secured to the foundation will vary from project to project. Always try to have as much bearing surface between the stringer and the foundation as possible. The bearing surface is simply that portion of the stringer that touches the foundation and supports the steps. Determine these bearing surfaces before you mark the tread and riser cuts.

5 Building the Foundation.
Lay a row of 8x8x16-inch concrete blocks equal to the width of the steps and fill them with concrete. When the concrete is stiff, but not hard, insert a 9-inch-long, 1/2-inch diameter anchor

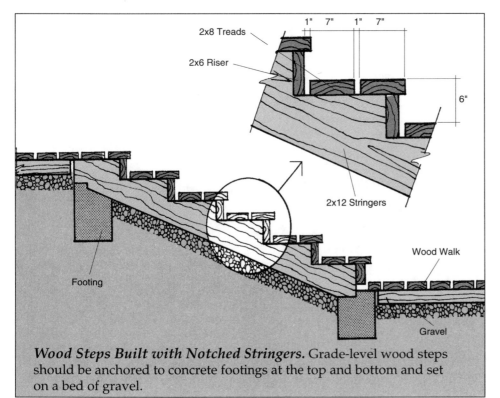

Wood Steps Built with Notched Stringers. Grade-level wood steps should be anchored to concrete footings at the top and bottom and set on a bed of gravel.

bolt as close as possible to each of the outside edges and another bolt in the middle; the bolt should go about 6 inches into the blocks and protrude about 3 inches above the top of the block. The bolts in each row will be anchored to a 2x6 plank laid across the top of the blocks. The planks provide a base in which notched stringers fit over and can be nailed. If your steps are wider than 4 feet, install anchor bolts no more than 2 feet on center, with an anchor at the outside edges of each step.

6 Planning the Notches. Brace one stringer temporarily in place with stakes or concrete blocks. Measure, locate and draw the tread and riser cuts. To draw the cuts, use a spirit level, a carpenter's square and a pencil. Mark the cuts, measuring off the tread depths with the carpenter's square. Use the level to be sure the carpenter's square is even. When you hold it along the tread line, you can mark both the tread and riser positions.

7 Cutting the Notches. Use a handsaw or rotary saw to saw out the notches on the 2x12 to form the tread and risers. Use the notched stringer as a pattern to cut the other stringers. Lay the notched stringer on the others and draw along the tread and riser notches.

8 Securing the Stringers. Reposition the stringer on the slope to be sure it can be secured to the foundation the way you want. Metal anchor clips, available at any building materials house, can be used to secure the stringers in position. Fasten the stringers to your foundation.

9 Attaching the Steps. Nail the tread and riser members to stringers.

Freestanding Steps

In some cases you may be dealing with a severe grade change that requires steps to bridge the grade change comfortably. In cases like this, you can build freestanding steps between the different grades.

1. Measure the grade change and slope distance and compute the tread and riser relationship. The foundation, in this example, is a concrete base at the foot of the slope and 4x4 pressure-treated posts at the top.

2. Set the 4x4 posts a minimum of 2 feet deep on a bed of gravel—this assumes a 3-foot vertical grade change. The posts should extend above the upper grade; cut them later to fit the stringer.

3. Pour concrete to 1 inch above grade at the posts and slope it away from the posts for proper drainage.

4. Pour the concrete base footing, using an oiled wood member form that has a notch for the stringer. After the concrete sets, remove the oiled member.

5. Secure the stringers to the top posts with four 3/8-inch diameter bolts at each post. Secure the stringers at the concrete base with metal anchor clips. You should have three stringers for steps that are 4 feet wide.

6. Trim the posts to the appropriate height. Notch the stringers and nail the treads and risers.

Railroad Tie or Log Steps

Railroad ties may be laid directly on the ground, but it is difficult to keep them neat and level without a base. Ties also can be laid on stringers for more stability. If a more informal, less hard-edged design is appropriate, lay logs directly on the ground and stake them from the sides at the ends or on the front (riser side). A gravel base is suggested for good drainage and longevity.

Laid on the Ground

1 First compute the slope rise. Figure the tread and riser relationship (see page 71). Then begin work on the excavation.

2 Use a pointed shovel to dig out rough treads and risers directly in the earth. Your logs, which should be pressure-treated, probably will vary somewhat in diameter. Excavate to size.

3 After you have the earth roughly shaped like steps, dig out the necessary depth so the tread surface of the logs will be at the level you want. If there is one side of a log that is more flat than another, then put that side up. Remember that your base must allow for the shape of the logs. Dig a trench large enough for the greatest circumference.

4 It is always wise to put 4 inches of gravel under any wood installed below grade. First add 4 inches to your excavation. The treads, from riser face to riser face, should be about 15 inches.

5 At the ends of the logs drive stakes 2 feet into the ground. The stakes must be long enough so that, after being driven into the ground, the tops of the stakes are even with the center of the ties (logs). Nail the stakes securely to the ties (logs). Use 16d or 20d (3½- or 4-inch) nails.

6 The surface of the log becomes part of the tread. However, since the logs curve, you will need to add some kind of filler. In areas informal enough for log steps, the best (most appropriate) filler is earth planted with a hardy ground cover. Other fillers, such as gravel, bark or wood chips, may be used. Cut brick or poured concrete also can be used. If you use brick, concrete or any hard surfacing material between the logs, cut and square off the logs where they will meet the hard surfaces. This will avoid a feather edge that would chip or break away in time.

Building Notched Stringers

Cross tie steps can be built with notched stringers. The installation techniques are:

■ Build the foundation as above;

■ Saw the notches in the stringers;

■ Lay the stringers on a bed of gravel;

■ Nail the stringers to the 2x6 plank over the foundation blocks;

■ Nail 2x6 risers to the stringers; then toenail the cross tie treads to the 2x6s (see bottom illustration).

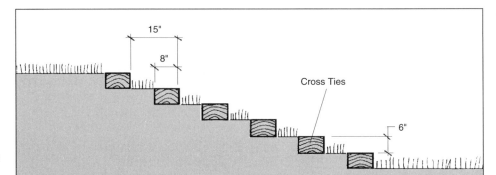

Installing on the Ground. Because they are heavy and stable, cross ties may be set into firm soil as step risers, and the top as part of the tread.

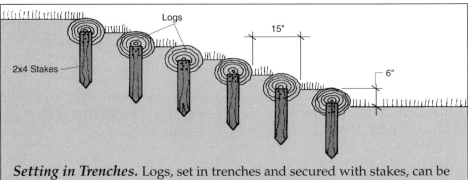

Setting in Trenches. Logs, set in trenches and secured with stakes, can be used as step risers in a natural landscaping plan.

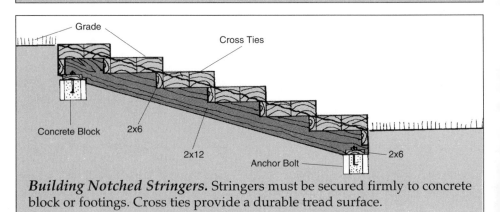

Building Notched Stringers. Stringers must be secured firmly to concrete block or footings. Cross ties provide a durable tread surface.

Designing Ramps

Ramps are used where a grade transition is too gentle for comfortable steps or too sloped for the run to be called a "walk." A surface with a pitch of more than 5 percent is considered a ramp. Of course, ramps are indispensable for the handicapped and the elderly, and they are convenient for any wheeled equipment that must be moved from level to level in the lawn. Ramps rarely replace stairs unless absolutely necessary, since some people find them hard to use.

Designing Stepped Ramps

Some grades will require a combination of a ramp and steps, called stepped ramps. The ramps may utilize single risers, pairs of risers or longer flights.

The selection of steps and/or ramps is a compromise between your terrain as it exists and the slope you have to give it to obtain good tread/riser relationships. For fairly gentle slopes, use stepped ramps with single risers; when you use stepped ramps with single risers, the grade should be no more than would lie on an imaginary line connecting the bottom of the upper riser of each pair of risers.

■ Ramps and stepped ramps should be the same width as the walks they meet when they reach ground level.

■ Risers should not be higher than 6 inches.

■ Treads (similar to landings) are most comfortable to walk on if they provide space for one or three comfortable paces—approximately 3 to 9 feet.

■ The maximum gradient for a ramp of any extended length should not exceed 1:12 (8.33%), not including curb ramps.

■ Handrails should extend a minimum 18 inches beyond top and bottom of ramp.

■ The minimum clear width of any ramp is 3 feet. Where ramps are heavily used by pedestrians and service deliveries, there should be sufficient width to accommodate both, or provisions made for alternate routes.

■ The bottom and top approach to a ramp should be clear and level for a distance of at least 5 feet, allowing for turning maneuvers by strollers, dollies or wheelchairs.

■ Plant materials should be located so that shadows do not prevent the sun from melting snow and ice on ramp surfaces.

■ Ramps should be designed to carry a minimum live load of 100 pounds per square foot.

■ Low curbs along the sides of ramps and landings (2 inches) should be provided as surfaces against which wheeled vehicles can turn their wheels in order to stop.

■ Ramps should be illuminated to an average maintained light level which ensures their safe use in darkness. It is important that the heel and toe of the ramp be particularly well illuminated.

■ Ramps should be maintained properly to keep them from being hazardous. Debris, snow and ice should be kept off the surface. Handrails must be securely fastened.

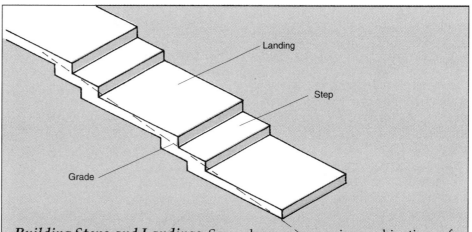

Building Steps and Landings. Some slopes may require combinations of steps and landings. The landings should allow the user to take at least three walking steps to maintain the most natural stride.

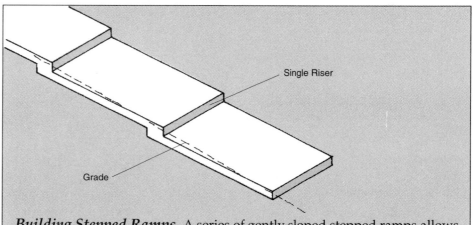

Building Stepped Ramps. A series of gently sloped stepped ramps allows control of the grade. The longer ramp treads allow for several steps to be taken on each for a more comfortable walk.

Adding a Footbridge

A footbridge is sometimes necessary in order to cross narrow depressions, creeks or other grade irregularities that you cannot, or do not wish, to level or fill.

A simple footbridge can be built with railroad ties for supports, 2x4s for decking and handrails, 4x4s for the posts, and 1/2-inch diameter anchor bolts to hold the structure in place. The following describes a 4-foot-wide bridge to span a 4-foot depression.

1 Positioning the Posts. Pairs of 4x4 posts on 4-foot centers are 7 feet on center on opposite sides of the depression. To be sure the post hole locations are square, lay the railroad ties across the depression as visually parallel and square as possible, and as close as possible to their final position.

On one side of the depression lay a 4-foot long 2x4 across the ends of the ties so that the 2x4 overhangs by 4 inches on each side. Using the outside edges of the ties as guides, stake the locations of the posts. Repeat on the other side. Remove ties and dig post holes to at least 18 inches deep.

2 Installing the Posts. Set the 4x4 posts in a bed of gravel. Pour concrete an inch or so above grade at the support post. Slope the concrete away from the post for good drainage. The posts should reach above the planned top level of the railroad ties. You can trim the posts after the railroad ties are in place. When the concrete sets, you are ready to lay the railroad ties.

Handrails

If the codes permit, you may wish to omit the handrail. For a handrail, extend the 4x4 supports above the top of the ties by 3 feet or to the height specified by the local code. Attach a 2x4 or 2x6 handrail, 2-inch side up. Handrails should be bolted with a minimum of two 3/8-inch diameter bolts at each post.

3 Installing Ties. Set the railroad ties against the support posts with the posts outside the ties; the ties will extend beyond the posts by 4 inches. Check the ties for level with a carpenter's level. Make minor adjustments by placing stones under the ties to level them. When the ties are level in the position relative to the posts, toenail them to the posts with 60d nails. Trim the posts off flush with the top of the ties.

4 Securing Ties and Decking. With the ties secured to the posts, drill two 5/8-inch holes through the posts and the ties where the posts meet the ties. Secure the ties to the posts with 1/2-inch diameter bolts.

Nail the 2x4 decking across the top of the ties, 2-inch side up. The 2x4s should overlap the ties 8 inches on each side. Keep the decking square by starting at either end of the ties with the first 2x4 flush with the end edges of the ties. Space the 2x4s 1 inch apart; use a spacer scrap to keep the distance equal. Toenail 2x4s to ties with 20d nails. The decking will be even more secure if you tie it all together by nailing 1x4 spacers between each 2x4 as you lay the 2x4 deck members. The 1x4s should be as long as the 2x4s.

Arched Bridge

If you would like a footbridge with a slight arch, use two 2x8s in place of each tie or landscaping member.

Cut the tops of the 2x8s in an arc that drops from the full width at the center down to 4 inches at the ends. Handrails can be arched in the same manner. Unless you have a good workshop, you would be better off using curve-sawed boards, available at some lumber companies.

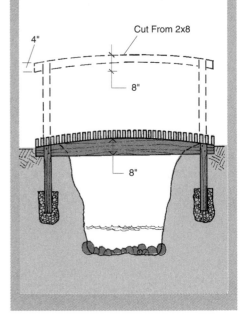

Adding a Footbridge. The support for the surface is provided by an 8x8 cross tie split lengthwise or two 4x8 landscaping timbers. The span members are bolted to 4x4 posts embedded in concrete. The walking surface is made of 2x4s.

Aggregates Crushed stone, gravel or other material used with cement and water to form concrete.

Air-entrained (concrete) Concrete which has been mixed with an admixture which causes tiny bubbles of air to be held in the mixture as the concrete sets. Air-entrained concrete is more workable and less vulnerable to frost.

Backfilling A process whereby earth is removed from an area to permit construction and is then returned to an area from whence it was removed.

Broom finishing Texturing of a concrete surface by stroking with a stiff broom while the concrete surface is still fresh.

Butter The process of applying mortar to brick or to other masonry units.

Cleats Blocks of wood, usually cut from 2x3 or 2x4, which are nailed to the inside of stringers for support, as for treads in a flight of stairs. The cleats support treads which are also attached to the stringers.

Common In brick the term refers to ordinary building brick as opposed to a specialty brick or other masonry unit such as firebrick or glazed brick.

Concrete Concrete consists of a mixture of cement, sand aggregate and water. Concrete continues to harden over a long period of time and becomes harder and stronger with age, although it is subject to cracking under the pressure of heat, cold and water.

Control Joints The lines cut into a concrete surface to ensure that when the slab cracks under normal water, frost, or heat pressures, it will crack only along these joint lines. These are cut to a depth of 1/4 to 1/5 the thickness of the slab, and placed every 4 to 10 feet in each direction. Failure to use control joints will cause uneven fracturing of the slab surface.

Darbying A smoothing of the surface of a concrete slab after initial leveling. Darbying is done with a darby tool or a long, smooth piece of lumber or steel.

Expansion joint A planned break in the continuous surface of a patio into which a compressible material has been placed to absorb pressure when the surface expands when heated. This joint prevents buckling or crumbling of the surface. Commonly used materials for expansion joints are wood, oakum or asphalt. Expansion joints are required wherever dissimilar materials adjoin since they will expand and contract at different rates.

Exposed aggregate A decorative surface treatment of concrete created when the smooth wearing surface of the concrete slab is washed away before the concrete has fully hardened to reveal a layer of coarse stone aggregate which has been embedded just below the surface.

Flashing A thin, impervious material placed in mortar joints to prevent water penetration, or in some cases to provide water drainage. Also referring to an impervious material used for the same purpose where deck ledger boards are attached to house walls.

Floating A finishing process in laying a concrete slab. After the surface has been leveled, a smooth piece of wood or steel is drawn across the surface of the wet concrete. Once the concrete has set to the point where there is no moisture apparent on the surface, a second floating is done to ensure that the final surface is level, smooth and unmarred.

Footing The portion of a foundation which directly transmits the structural load to the ground. For decks, footings are usually placed only where the posts will be located. Footings also are required for support columns for overhead cover and for some fence posts.

Isolation joint The same type of joint as an expansion joint.

Joints In masonry, the mortar-filled spaces between masonry units.

Ledger A horizontal board attached to the side of a house or other wall to support the deck on overhead cover. It is secured with lag screws and expansion shields to masonry walls and with carriage bolts or spikes to wooden walls.

Masonry Brick, tile, stone, block, or other material, usually small enough to be handled by one man, that bonds together with mortar to form a permanent structure.

Mason's line A length of twine which is held at each end by an L-shaped block. The line can be stretched tight and is used as a straightedge guide; permitting the mason to check the evenness of the course being laid.

Mortar An elastic mixture of cement, sand and water which is used to bond units of masonry together.

Nominal dimension A dimension which is greater then the actual dimension of lumber or masonry. In lumber, supposedly the wood size before it has been milled. A brick nominal size usually allows for a 1/2 inch mortar joint to give the full nominal dimension.

Patterns In masonry there are many regularly used methods of laying units which create recognizable patterns which have been named: i.e. running bond and basket weave.

Pavers Man-made units, frequently identified as "paving bricks" which are either brick or molded concrete. There are many types, styles and sizes. Some interlock in patterns and when properly set in a base of sand or concrete will withstand a great deal of weight.

Plumb On a straight vertical line. A wall which is plumb is straight up and down with no lean. When constructing a wall or deck or roof, plumb must be checked regularly to ensure vertical stability.

Portland cement A type of cement (not a brand name), this combination of elements is largely lime and silica and is basic to making concrete and mortar.

Railroad ties Thick, square lengths of timber which are set into the bed of a railroad track and to which the tracks are attached. Railroad ties are durable and are frequently used in landscaping

Reinforcing In masonry structures, rods, mini-trusses or metal ties which reach from one wythe or course to another through the mortar for greater stability and permanence.

Retaining walls A wall built to hold back a slope of ground. The retaining wall must be designed to withstand enormous pressure and requires substantial footing to redistribute pressure to ground. Most retaining walls require weep holes to relieve buildup of ground water pressure.

Risers In stairs, the board which supports the front edge of a tread. A cleat-supported tread can exist without a riser in a flight of open stairs.

Spacers Uniformly sized pieces of plywood, or nails or other material, set between construction components to maintain a set, even distance between units during placement or nailing.

Stringers Wood or metal supports for a flight of stairs, running at an angle from the lower to the upper level.

Tread On a flight of stairs, the level surface on which one steps.

Troweling A final finishing of the surface of a concrete slab, for an extremely smooth face on the slab. In bricklaying, the application of the mortar, also "buttering."

Weep hole A hole in a retaining wall that allows water to seep through and thus relieve pressure against the wall.